NEW ENGLAND REMEMBERS

The Hurricane of 1938

Aram Goudsouzian

CE

Commonwealth Editions
Beverly, Massachusetts

This book is dedicated to my parents, Nishan and Mary Goudsouzian.
They taught me all the important things.

Library of Congress Cataloging-in-Publication Data
Goudsouzian, Aram.
 The hurricane of 1938 / Aram Goudsouzian.
 p. cm. — (New England remembers)
 Includes bibliographical references and index.
 ISBN 1-889833-75-4
 1. Hurricanes—New England—History—20th century. 2. Hurricanes—New York (State) —Long Island—History—20th century. 3. New England—History—20th century. 4. Long Island (N.Y.)—History—20th century. I. Title. II. Series.
 F9.G68 2004
 974'.042—dc22   2004011485

Cover and interior design by Laura McFadden Design, Inc.
laura.mcfadden@rcn.com
Printed in the United States of America

Printed in the United States

Commonwealth Editions
an imprint of Memoirs Unlimited, Inc.
266 Cabot Street, Beverly, Massachusetts 01915
www.commonwealtheditions.com

The New England Remembers series
Robert J. Allison, General Editor
The Hurricane of 1938 by Aram Goudsouzian
The Big Dig by James Aloisi

Cover photos: (*Front*) The lower harbor of New London, Connecticut; (*back*) Bourne Bridge, Bourne, Massachusetts. Both photos are used courtesy of the Boston Public Library.

The "New England Remembers" logo features a photo of the Thomas Pickton House, Beverly, Massachusetts, used courtesy of the Beverly Historical Society.

CONTENTS

FOREWORD

IT KILLED MORE PEOPLE than the San Francisco earthquake and the Chicago fire combined. The hurricane of 1938 struck suddenly on September 21, and by the time the storm was over, 680 people were dead and thousands more homeless; downtown Providence had been flooded twice; 72 million feet of power lines were down, and 88 percent of New Englanders were without electricity; countless trees were uprooted, and 175 churches damaged—six of them utterly destroyed. Though the coast of Rhode Island was hit hardest, a survivor in New Hampshire's White Mountains reported that only in "certain shell-torn woods in France" during the Great War had he seen worse devastation.

Aram Goudsouzian tells the story of the worst natural catastrophe in New England's history. But this is a story not only of a big storm, but of the many people who endured it. The storm struck as the men, women, and children of New England were enduring the calamity of the Great Depression, and as they anxiously watched the gathering cataclysm in Europe. In telling individual stories of heroism and cowardice, tragedy and redemption, Goudsouzian brings the storm vividly to life.

The Hurricane of 1938 is the first in a series of books—New England Remembers—about people and events that have shaped New England's history. Written with economy and insight, these books capture the unique character of New England. The Hurricane of 1938 struck before satellites tracked storms or forecasters gave them names. But from the coast of Connecticut and Rhode Island, to the mountains of New Hampshire and Vermont, New England remembers the Hurricane of 1938.

Robert J. Allison, Series Editor
Boston, Massachusetts

CHAPTER ONE

Onset

ROUND NOON on September 21, 1938, George Burghard found water frothing through the floor of his summer cottage's garage. A wealthy man from the Upper East Side of Manhattan, he had rented the cottage on Westhampton Beach, a sandy ribbon stretching along the southern shore of Long Island. To the north, between the dunes and the mainland, was normally placid Moriches Bay. To the south was the Atlantic Ocean.

The foaming water surprised Burghard. His house was two hundred feet from the ocean's edge, protected from the breakers by an eight-foot dune. Moreover, his stately cottage had a concrete foundation and protective wooden bulkheads on the surf side. He assumed that northeast winds were blowing bay water into his basement garage. To his surprise, he tasted seawater.

Burghard was surprised, but not worried. He thought nothing of it when, an hour later, he heard on the radio that "the West Indies hurricane is in the mid-Atlantic." Clearly, a storm was brewing, but in his lifetime no hurricane had hit Long Island. Anyway, the radio announcer sounded so nonchalant. Burghard drew no connection between the hurricane at sea and the water in his basement.

That soon changed. Within two hours, the winds had shifted eastward and built to speeds of ninety miles per hour. George's wife, Mabel, left the sunporch, where she had been sewing with her back to a large window. Moments later the window shattered and shards of glass surged in, followed by rain and sand. In the basement, two and a half feet of swirling whitecaps flooded the garage and servants' quarters. Uncomprehending of the storm's magnitude, Carl and Selma Dalin, the Burghards' elderly butler and maid, thought they would be safe spending the night on the third floor.

By this time a huge wave had crashed over the dune. The second big wave, a four-foot mass of white water moving at roughly twenty miles per hour, pulled a bathhouse off its foundation. When George and Carl waded into the basement to retrieve clothes for the night, another wave swept through and carried George down the hallway, depositing him near his garage.

Across a meadow, the Coast Guard's Potunk Station was nearly submerged. John Avery, the guardsman on duty, fought through the watery wreckage at around 3:30 P.M. to reach the Burghards. "Well, lad," asked George, "do you think it's getting better or worse?" It was getting worse. The entire protective dune was on the brink of collapse. They decided to abandon the house. They would walk a half-mile east along Dune Road, where they would cross a bridge to the mainland. The Dalins, both in their sixties, seemed stunned. Even George, gathering himself for the march, left behind his watch and keys but brought two tickets to the next day's tennis match at Forest Hills.

At 4:00 P.M. Avery, the Burghards, the Dalins, the fox terrier Bitzie, and the cocker spaniel Peter began their exodus. Walking along fences and hedges, grabbing onto telephone poles and each other for support, dodging projectile planks and timbers, they braced themselves against green towers of waves. The wind now blew over a hundred miles per hour. The sky was dark, the air thick with humidity, the surging water almost tropically warm. The storm possessed a barely comprehensible force. Behind them waves pounded the Coast Guard station, finally washing it and its tall steel lookout tower into the bay. Selma Dalin held fast to a telephone pole and refused to let go. Seventy-five feet behind everyone else, her husband, Carl, sat motionless on a fence, staring at the water below him.

After fifteen minutes Avery and the Burghards realized that they would never make the mainland on foot. Then came a lucky break. Their neighbors' bathhouse lifted off its foundation, struck some telephone poles, and broke up. A large flat piece landed by them. George, Mabel, and the Coast Guardsman climbed aboard with Bitzie and Peter, but the Dalins refused to budge. The next wave washed their impromptu raft into the bay. Remarkably, the winds had driven so much bay water onto the mainland that for a two-hundred-foot stretch, in between waves, the raft landed on the dry floor of the bay. But every six-foot wall of white water washed them farther away from the dunes. The wind pushed them west, and for some time they feared that they would drift through an inlet out to sea. They dodged a flotilla of bobbing cars, houses, and even a fifty-foot fuel tank. Their raft grew flimsy. When they tried to put the dogs on another piece of debris, Peter and Bitzie swam back playfully.

Their raft was starting to sink when a huge chunk of a smashed-up house floated by. They sidestepped upturned nails to board this larger and better raft, and they used splintered chunks of wood to paddle toward Oneck Point, maneuvering among wave-propelled, sharply angled remnants of houses. "The bay was like the ocean," Mabel later told the *New York Times*. "It was a wild, raging sea, filled with screaming people and all kinds of debris." Above them, a flock of ducks tried to fly into the wind, but were instead getting pushed backward at about forty miles per hour.

Finally the party landed ashore in a clump of berry bushes. Wrecked roofs and walls, churning behind them in the bay, seemed ready to wash over them. Avery hustled Mabel to higher ground, and the cocker spaniel Peter swam behind them. Bitzie hopped onto another roof and floated away, and the Burghards never saw their terrier again. They waded across a road three feet under water to reach the high ground of a golf course fairway. Avery then left George and Mabel to help a hysterical woman whose two babies were stranded in her nearby home. For his actions that day, Coast Guardsman Avery later received a commendation for bravery.

The Burghards marched down the fairway toward the village of Westhampton. Mabel still held her pocketbook, despite a sprained wrist and ankle. At times the wind almost lifted her off her feet, and George had to hold her down. When they reached a dry road, they hitched a ride with a man searching for his family. Fallen trees and utility poles blocked countless roads. Finally they reached the Montauk Highway, a clear path into Westhampton. By evening the winds had slowed, but the center of town was six feet under water; the storm had carved an inlet straight into the village. The Burghards took shelter in a home on high ground with a hot stove, coffee, and brandy. Their fellow refugees raised their eyebrows when the bruised, disheveled pair claimed that they and their dog had floated across Moriches Bay from Westhampton Beach.

After midnight, George set out across Westhampton's tree-choked streets back to the country club—now an improvised morgue. There he met Carl

A ruined home along the southern coast of Long Island (courtesy of the East Hampton Library)

Dalin's son Alvin, and together they identified the butler's body. Carl had broken his leg, drowned, and washed ashore at 9:30 P.M., near where the Burghards had landed. His wife, Selma, was found at 2:00 A.M. a half-mile east. George and Alvin identified her body as dawn broke.

The next day George and Mabel returned to Westhampton Beach. Of the 179 houses on the dunes, only twenty-six remained. One day before, it had been a sandy playground for the wealthy. Now it stunk of mud and was littered with piles of splintered homes, waterlogged cars, uprooted trees, and smashed furniture. The Burghards' roof had landed across the bay, on the golf course. A shingle from the house had pierced the side of a Coast Guard lifeboat. One of George's vests was found on the mainland, twenty feet high in a tree. Mabel's riding boots floated a half-mile away from each other. And where their cottage once stood, George and Mabel found only part of a loudspeaker, a card table (with three legs intact), their neighbor's beach umbrella, one of Carl Dalin's sweaters, and the kitchen sink.

THE BURGHARDS' EXTRAORDINARY STORY revealed the larger power, tragedy, and surprise behind the Great New England Hurricane of 1938. This tempest produced peak steady winds of 121 miles per hour, and the Blue Hill

Observatory near Boston recorded one gust at 186 miles per hour. Barometers dipped remarkably low, to below 28. Seawater killed vegetation twenty miles inland, tides rose up to seventeen feet above mean high water, and ocean salt sprayed windows as far north as Montpelier, Vermont, 120 miles from the nearest coast. As the Burghards' tale indicates, the hurricane first hit land on Long Island. The storm thus earned a second nickname: The Long Island Express.

It was an express train of destruction, moving fifty miles an hour through southeastern New England and up the Connecticut River Valley. It uprooted or damaged 275 million trees, knocked down 20,000 miles of power and telephone lines, and ruined 26,000 automobiles. According to the Red Cross, the hurricane destroyed 6,933 coastal cottages, 1,991 homes, 2,605 boats, 2,369 barns, and 7,438 other buildings. It caused an estimated $400 million in damage. One accepted calculation places the total number of deaths at 680. At least two previous storms—at Galveston, Texas, in 1900 and at Lake Okeechobee, Florida, in 1928—had killed more people. But New England's dense residential patterns and developed economy made the Hurricane of 1938 the costliest natural disaster in American history up to that time.

"That was when I stopped believing in God!" one survivor recalled almost forty years later. The storm seemed so vicious, so arbitrary in its choice of victims that some abandoned faith. Moreover, it felled the great symbols of New England: hundreds of church steeples, the graceful anchors of the region's town greens, crashed to the ground, in some cases landing point first on front lawns. The storm even reshaped the earth itself, creating new inlets and carving chunks out of coastline. Yet others saw the hurricane as the work of God—an angry, Old Testament God. One Long Island farmer asked a hand why he thought God sent such calamity upon innocents. The laborer admitted that he did not know, "unless He just wanted us to know He was Boss."

Whether a higher power was at work or not, the hurricane's aftermath resembled a scene from a ghastly surrealist painting: neighborhoods reduced to matchsticks, cars serenely languishing on flooded streets, gnarled railroad tracks spiraling to nowhere, sailboats grounded in downtown shopping districts, streets and sidewalks mutated into shattered ribbons of concrete. For many survivors, the eeriest part was the sound. "It was like nothing else," wrote Ernest Clowes, an observer for the U.S. Weather Bureau in Bridgehampton, Long Island. He heard three main chords: a deep rumble of the sea, a high-pitched whinny through the treetops, and a third, most powerful note—"a steady, almost organ-like note of such intensity that it seemed as if the whole atmosphere were in harmonic vibration. No sound rose above it. It was something one not only heard but felt to the core of one's being." Trees could be toppling, windows smashing, houses splintering—and one might hear none of it.

❧   ❧   ❧

THE HURRICANE OF 1938 ARRIVED AT A CROSSROADS in American history. The nation was nine years into the Great Depression. The average American family lived on less than $1,500 a year, and that family did not own a home. The crisis had so crushed the economy that it had fomented doubts about the bedrock American institutions of capitalism and democracy. By destroying small farms and leaving factory workers unemployed, the hurricane exacerbated the region's hardships, especially for those low on the economic totem pole.

Was the Depression a type of hurricane? President Herbert Hoover employed that very imagery in the years after the stock market crash of 1929. Holding firm to his faith in the American economy, he saw the Depression as a test of individual character—if he could sustain the people's confidence, then the nation would rebound. In a June 1931 address in Indianapolis, he dismissed proposals of radical legislation: "Such views are as accurate as the belief that we can exorcise a Caribbean hurricane by statutory law." The next year, while accepting the Republican presidential nomination, he bemoaned that "beginning eighteen months ago, the worldwide storm grew to hurricane force." By likening the crisis to a hurricane, Hoover recognized its severity. But the metaphor also suggested that the economy was in a normal downturn—an inevitable product of natural forces. Hurricanes may destroy, but they also pass, leaving only the structures on the firmest foundations.

Alas, this hurricane was not passing. Their enduring poverty compelled the American people to reject Hoover and elect Franklin D. Roosevelt. The new president led a fundamental redefinition of the federal government's place in the daily life of its citizens. His New Deal did not end the Great Depression, but it did establish massive federal programs to promote security in such diverse realms as finance, housing, and agriculture. "That brief span of years," reflected the historian David Kennedy, "constituted one of only a handful of episodes in American history when substantial and lasting social change has occurred—when the country was, in measurable degree, remade." The 1930s witnessed a restructuring of the federal government's relationship to ordinary Americans—a development with direct relevance in the hurricane's aftermath, when New Deal agencies funneled millions of dollars to the stricken zones, providing relief and employing thousands of workers in dire need.

Hoover's failed analogy aside, hurricanes still possessed a certain mythic power in the American consciousness. The 1937 film *The Hurricane*, produced by Samuel Goldwyn and directed by John Ford, was a huge commercial success. The film examines the relationship between the law-and-order French colonial governor and a South Pacific native who keeps escaping prison. After an hour and a half of corny melodrama, the final fifteen minutes saves the movie: A hurricane (spectacularly reproduced at Goldwyn's studio) allows the native to rescue not only his own family but also the governor's wife. The governor then grants freedom to his heroic foe. The hurricane exposed the true character of both men.

In September 1938, as the actual hurricane struck New England, another crisis loomed. In Europe, democracy was in peril. To achieve Adolf Hitler's vision of a fascist pan-German empire, Nazi Germany had already swallowed Austria. Hitler now demanded the Czechoslovakian territory of the Sudetenland. On the morning of the hurricane, Czechoslovakia faced a decision: submit to Hitler or face a German invasion. Britain and France urged submission; the United States condemned Nazi belligerence but stayed its isolationist course. Though an ocean away, the Czechoslovakian crisis would contribute to a certain historical amnesia about the Hurricane of 1938, as American attention drifted away from the regional disaster to the world-encompassing zero hour.

The Nazi aggression would continue and lead to World War II. And just as the Great Depression had spawned a massive rearrangement of domestic politics, so too would World War II usher in an era of American international leadership. Crises have such power. The Hurricane of 1938 was no exception. On Long Island and in New England, the storm produced a momentary anarchy. As in Goldwyn's movie, the storm exposed the true character of its victims: man at his most noble, at his most base, even at his most ordinary. The storm further reoriented relationships—not just among the region's people, but between people and technology, people and government, people and nature, even people and higher powers.

Those braving the winds, waves, floods, and fires of September 21, however, were focused not on the calamity's historical impact but on their own survival. And survival was a struggle, one that sometimes relied on luck, sometimes on ingenuity, sometimes even on heroism. It very rarely resulted from foresight and planning, because almost no one knew that a hurricane was coming.

CHAPTER TWO

Into New York

N ATURE IS NOT TO BE trifled with when she is in one of her angrier moods," the *New York Times* declared in a September 21, 1938, editorial titled "Hurricane." A storm had recently threatened to strike Florida. "If New York and the rest of the world have been so well informed about the cyclone," averred the newspaper, "it is because of an admirably organized meteorological service." In an implicit jab at the fascist aggression plaguing Europe, the editorial praised the spirit of international cooperation in the name of science. Ships at sea had reported weather data regardless of political affiliation or economic gain, and the U.S. Weather Bureau had issued the appropriate warnings to those along the nation's southeastern coast. Luckily, the hurricane had turned out to sea.

Few essays have ever been so ironically ill-timed. That very day the hurricane ripped apart Long Island and New England, and virtually none of its victims had prepared for the disaster. Behind that tragedy lay a unique set of meteorological conditions—circumstances that not only forged a massive hurricane, but also sent it atypically northward, devastating an unsuspecting region and surprising the nation's best forecasters.

ℰ   ℰ   ℰ

ATLANTIC HURRICANES FORM IN THE "DOLDRUMS" near the Cape Verde Islands, off the coast of West Africa. In this belt, the equatorial sun heats the ocean's surface, causing evaporation. The column of hot, humid air then ascends and cools. Water vapor condenses into water drops, releasing energy and generating heat, which keeps the air rising. The air pressure at the surface plunges—the signature of a developing hurricane. Strong winds form when air rushes in to fill the void left by the column of ascending air. Because the earth rotates, these winds follow a circular pattern: counterclockwise in the northern hemisphere, clockwise in the southern hemisphere. Given proper conditions—humid air, constant winds, warm surface water—these spiraling winds can accelerate, and the system can become a hurricane.

On September 4, 1938, a French meteorological station in the Sahara detected a cluster of spiraling winds in the doldrums, a somewhat common occurrence. Only one in ten of these formations develops into a hurricane. But by September 10, the system had evolved into a tropical storm, with wind speeds around forty miles per hour. The U.S. Weather Bureau tracked the storm as it moved west across the Atlantic, pushed by the prevailing easterly winds of the tropics.

Established by President Ulysses Grant in 1870 as a branch of the army, the Weather Bureau later came under the jurisdiction of the Department of Agriculture and then the Department of Commerce. In 1935, the bureau established branches in Jacksonville, New Orleans, Boston, and San Juan. Unfortunately, the government could not afford to send its own men on storm-tracking aerial excursions; as the *New York Times* editorial indicated, forecasters relied on voluntary reports of data. Ships radioed their observations to shore stations, and those stations telegraphed the information to the Weather Bureau. Meteorologists needed about an hour to process these reports. Not for another generation would the bureau possess the modern tools of meteorology: radar, jet planes, satellites with television equipment. "Its chief devices then," wrote the historian William Manchester, "were the sixteenth-century thermometer, the seventeenth-century mercurial barometer, and the medieval weathervane."

On September 16, a Brazilian freighter encountered the storm about ten degrees west of the Caribbean islands. Spinning across humid water, the system had pulled more vapor into its orbit and grown in power. The wind speeds now approached a hundred miles per hour, more than enough to earn an upgrade from "tropical storm" to "hurricane." On September 19, as the system curved northwest off the coast of the Bahamas, the winds reached speeds of over 160 miles per hour. The Jacksonville office issued a warning that a hurricane might strike Florida.

In 1935, the Great Labor Day Hurricane had killed 428 people in Jacksonville. This time, storm-hardened Floridians took no chances. They stocked up on candles, stored water, and barricaded windows. The Red Cross set up shelters, and telephone and power companies prepared reserves of emergency workers. Many vacationers boarded trains back to New England. One Stockbridge, Massachusetts, man wired home that he would extend his stay in Florida, so that he could experience a real hurricane.

Luckily, the prevailing westerly winds at higher latitudes kept the storm at bay. By the morning of September 20, the hurricane was moving almost directly north. The threat was presumably over. According to conventional wisdom, the winds would push the hurricane to the northeast, where it would dissipate in the colder waters of the mid-Atlantic. Already the wind speeds had begun to diminish. The Jacksonville office issued storm warnings along the Carolina coast, and then it passed responsibility to headquarters in Washington. The *New York Times* penned its editorial praising scientific progress, international cooperation, and man's respect of natural forces.

But the Washington bureau bungled its job. The office lagged behind its European counterparts, who were using new forecasting techniques based upon air mass analysis and the influence of weather fronts. A confidential government report issued in January 1938 lamented that the Forecast Division lacked "any plan or method for systematic training of would-be official forecasters." The report continued: "It is a sorry state of affairs when candidates for such a responsible position are obliged to shift for themselves, picking up scraps of information as best they can."

Yet even without sophisticated training and technology, a forecaster could have observed the existing data and predicted the hurricane's path. Three conditions suggested the outcome. First, on the morning of September 21, the RMS *Carinthia* was battered by gale-force winds while heeding the bureau's early warnings and hugging the Virginia coast. The captain also reported an alarmingly low barometric reading of 27.85 inches, indicating that the hurricane's eye was closer to shore than predicted. Second, a high-pressure zone hovered over the Allegheny Mountains, west of the North Atlantic coast. Third, ships off Cape Henry, Virginia, reported temperatures ten degrees higher than those closer to shore—an indication that the "Bermuda High" was at least ten degrees north of its normal position.

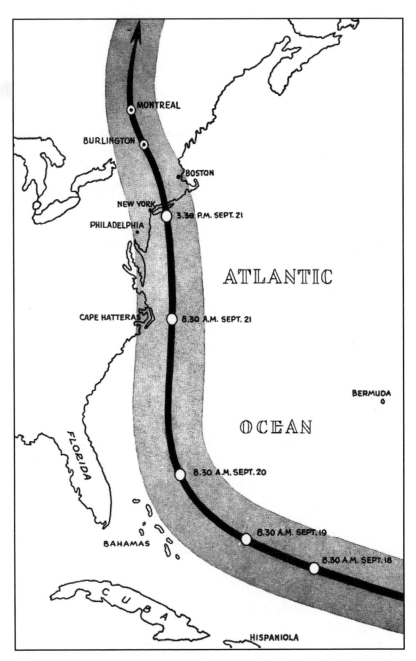

This map of the hurricane's path appeared in a special edition of the New Bedford Standard-Times. *All time shown is Daylight Saving Time.*

Charles Pierce, a twenty-eight-year-old rookie in the Washington Weather Bureau, pieced together this puzzle. Filling in for two off-duty forecasters at a noon meeting, Pierce argued that the hurricane would stay sandwiched between the high-pressure zones to the east and west, following a tongue of low pressure that extended straight northward. He accurately mapped the storm's eventual path through New England. But chief forecaster Charles Mitchell, backed by his senior advisers, overruled Pierce. In Mitchell's long and celebrated tenure, no hurricane had struck even the southern tip of New Jersey. Moreover, the current storm was weakening.

At 10:00 A.M. the Washington bureau had downgraded the hurricane to a tropical storm. At 12:30 P.M. it only warned of whole gale winds, which meant wind speeds up to seventy-five miles per hour. By the time the forecasters recognized that the hurricane was heading straight north—picking up strength and speed—it had already struck land.

Dr. Charles Clark, the Weather Bureau's acting chief, later defended his forecasters, calling the storm a "freak" that "did not follow the usual pattern." That was true. But hurricanes had hit New England before. The Massachusetts Bay Colony governor John Winthrop wrote of an August 1635 storm—barely five years after the settlement of Boston—that "blew with such violence, with abundance of rain, that it blew down many hundreds of trees, near the towns, and drove the ships from their anchors." In Narragansett Bay, tides rose "fourteen feet higher than ordinary, and drowned eight Indians flying from their wigwams." The Great September Gale of 1815 wreaked similar havoc: destroying orchards, killing cattle, whipping ninety-foot sprays of water from the Charles River. That hurricane so inspired a precocious six-year-old named Oliver Wendell Holmes that he later composed this doggerel:

It chanced to be our washing day,
And all our things were drying;
The storm came roaring through the lines;
And set them all a flying;
I saw the skirts and petticoats
Go riding off like witches;
I lost ah! Bitterly I wept,—
I lost my Sunday breeches!

In the 123 years since the Great September Gale of 1815, the region had developed an industrial economy, modern cities, and densely packed populations. There was more to lose than Sunday finery.

~ ~ ~

THE HURRICANE OF 1938 SPARED THE JERSEY SHORE, New York City, and upstate New York only by comparison. The storm's eye passed over Long Island, and those to the east of it suffered the worst. To the west, the average wind speed generally stayed below seventy-five miles per hour, the minimum requisite speed for an official hurricane. But the tempest was the mid-Atlantic's most severe in fifty years, and it left a deep bruise.

Thirty-foot waves and torrential winds destroyed the Jersey Shore's boardwalks, fishing piers, and pavilions. The bridge connecting the island of Brigantine to Atlantic City collapsed, and more than two thousand people were stranded for the night. Waves submerged Bay Head and spilled into Barnegat Bay, carrying away the boardwalk and dozens of beach cottages. Inland, the winds plucked off farmers' tomato and apple crops. Seaside estates and golf courses in New York's Westchester County sustained flooding.

A man reported from Times Square that, at 3:00 P.M., "one was hardly aware of anything more than a big blow." Yet by that evening, the storm had briefly crippled New York City. Ships smashed against piers, and fallen trees in city parks caused roughly $450,000 in damage. Sewers in the Bronx clogged with debris, and some neighborhoods in the outer boroughs lost electric power in the early afternoon. The East River flooded three blocks inland at 133rd Street, inundating the Hell Gate plant of the Consolidated Edison Company. That evening, for periods ranging from fifteen minutes to a few hours, all of the Bronx and parts of Manhattan sat in darkness.

Ferries and railroads had to suspend service, and the roads connecting the city to Westchester County, New Jersey, and Pennsylvania did not all open until late the next afternoon. New York City narrowly averted a milk shortage. Yet the city was relatively lucky. Only one man died there, an unidentified hitch-hiker who tried to wade to higher ground from the middle of a flooded street in Queens. An observer, stranded on the roof of his car, saw the man drift off and drown in the twilight.

In the city and in western Long Island, the strongest winds came from the north and northwest. On Long Island's south shore, debris from the pavilions at Jones Beach blew south, into the Atlantic. From Huntington to Manhasset Bay on the north shore, the waterfront absorbed collisions from wind-propelled boats. The J. P. Morgan estate in Glen Cove suffered extensive damage. New York City mayor Fiorello LaGuardia's wife, Marie, sat out the storm from her Northport cottage's second floor, while furniture floated downstairs.

The hurricane took a heavier toll as one went east. *New York Times* correspondent Russell Owen drove across northern Long Island in the midst of the storm. His first evidence of real devastation was on the Jericho State Parkway, where wind gusts shifted his car and fallen trees impeded his progress. By the time he was halfway across the island, his headlights cut barely twenty yards into rain-swept darkness. At the mouth of the North Fork, he was bypassing blocked streets by driving across lawns and fields. In Southold, chestnuts flew off a tree and through a home's windows, "riddling them like machine gun bullets." After five hours, he was five miles from his destination of Greenport. Alas, "where a well-paved State highway ordinarily lay, now the Sound intervened in all its formidable majesty." Windswept water had isolated the tip of the North Fork.

Long Island's southern coast, especially its eastern half from Fire Island to the South Fork, was even more devastated. Two conditions explain this locus of destruction. First, a northbound hurricane's winds are strongest on its eastern side, as prevailing westerly winds intensify the counterclockwise gusts spiraling up from the south. Second, the southern shore endured the "storm surge"—a tidal wave, except that a tidal wave is technically caused by earthquakes. These surges happen when hurricane winds push water into the storm's center. At sea, the water can spread out. But as the ocean floor rises near land, the water cannot flow away. The waves pile up on each other, then crash upon the shore. Typically these storm-driven waves cause about three-fourths of hurricane-related deaths. In the previous century, storm surges had killed appalling numbers: two hundred thousand in Backergunge, India, in 1876 and three hundred thousand in Haifong, China, in 1881.

During the Hurricane of 1938, the storm surges struck east of the eye, where the strongest winds, pushing up from the south, drove into the exposed coastline. The effect was devastating. After more than half the storm had passed, and after winds and waves had already debilitated the shore, a massive mountain of water descended upon the coast. Toni Stevens, then a Westhampton schoolchild, later described "a solid, square, gray wall of water about thirteen feet high, slowly but steadily devouring the dividing line between sky and grass. It was hypnotic." After the first big wave, others followed. They ingested the beach communities built on the sandy islands along Long Island's southern shore. Seawater weighs sixty-four pounds per cubic foot. The jolt from the first surge registered on seismographs in Alaska.

The waves began assaulting Fire Island around 3:00 P.M. By evening the island's Coast Guard station had washed into Great South Bay, and the ocean had cut an eight-foot-deep channel between Saltaire and Fair Harbor. Only twenty-five of 150 cottages in Saltaire remained standing. A Coast Guard icebreaker carried seventy-five people to safety, and a ferryboat captain rescued another forty-three. About forty others insisted on riding out the storm in a community center, even after the icebreaker returned and anchored off the coast, ready to evacuate them if necessary. Only six of Fair Harbor's seventy-five houses survived. Across the bay in Mastic Beach, the tides swept away a man's artificial legs. A week later the legs were found six miles away in East Moriches, lying side by side.

ℓ   ℓ   ℓ

WESTHAMPTON BEACH, where George and Mabel Burghard had their summer home, was hit hardest. This strip of exposed beach, typically a summer Shangri-La for the wealthy, endured the fiercest winds and a crippling storm surge. The exclusive beach clubs and stately cottages along Dune Road crumbled into Moriches Bay, causing $2 million in property loss. One month later, Westhampton Beach counted twenty-eight dead and four missing.

In the community of Pond Point, about thirty refugees fought through ankle-deep water and headwinds to reach high ground at the Pond Point Garage, where they gathered small boats and oars. The gusts first blew from the east. A lull then ensued as the eye of the storm passed. (Further east in Brentwood, someone recorded a fifty-minute pause, suggesting that the eye measured as wide as forty-three miles). When the wind resumed—this time from the southwest, and even stronger—it blew homes off their foundations. The refugees jumped into the boats and sailed across the bay. Only two boats reached the mainland without capsizing.

James Harris tried to bring three older women, including his mother, across Moriches Bay from Pond Point. The boat overturned, killing one woman immediately. Harris clung to the boat with one arm and held his mother with the other. The other woman held onto the boat until they approached shore; then fatigue overtook her, and she drowned. Harris and his mother washed up on shore, climbed atop the roof of a flooded bathhouse, and collapsed in exhaustion.

Tot Greene, the wife of a millionaire broker, had been hosting an impromptu children's party at her summer home on the east end of Westhampton Beach. After lunch the northeast wind came up, "angry and stronger than ever, making a horrible sound like a woman keening hysterically." The garage doors tore off their hinges. Mrs. Greene tried to bring in some laundry, but the winds pinned her against the house. The telephone died as she started to call parents to retrieve their children. Soon electricity and water were gone, too. A young couple, their children, their servants, and three furniture movers came from across the street, and everyone retreated to the Greenes' attic. The winds shifted and sharpened, and a baby nurse cried, "We will all be drowned!" The concrete porches on both sides of the two-story, million-dollar Greene cottage provided some protection. But as the water crept to the attic floor, they watched a neighbor's house float into the bay.

Meanwhile, Tot's husband, Norvin, was riding the train out from New York City. The crew and some passengers had to axe and saw fallen trees before pushing them off the tracks. A derailed train in Speonk finally stopped the slow journey. Greene hired a taxi, but more fallen trees halted his progress toward Westhampton. He walked to Six Corners, looking for a ride to Dune Road. "There are no dunes," he was told. "They have disappeared." He heard a rumor that his family had drowned in the bay. The beaches along Dune Road were inaccessible: roads and bridges were knocked out, and sunken cars and floating debris guarded the waters. The Coast Guard refused to ferry him there.

Norvin could not procure a boat until early Thursday morning. He feared the worst as he waded to the dunes, trudged through wet sand, and surveyed the devastation. Then he saw a party of nineteen people, including his wife and children. Their attic shelter had survived. After the hurricane had passed, they had spent the night in a neighbor's stone home. The children had eaten ketchup sandwiches for dinner, and they had slept bundled together in curtains. Soon after reuniting, they heard a radio broadcast that Mrs. Norvin Greene, her two children, and their party guests had washed out to sea. Friday's *New York Sun* reported them "swept away in the deluge. Not a single member of the gathering at the party was seen again." Relatives had already heard the bulletin and abandoned hope. Norvin Greene, gulping down his first-ever early-morning Scotch, happily knew otherwise.

A devastated village in southern Long Island (courtesy of the East Hampton Library)

Others in Westhampton had remarkable stories, too. Two maids and a two-year-old baby passed the ordeal in a house whose roof had blown off. The roof of a Westhampton home split in two, leaving a husband on one piece and his wife on the other; they drifted in separate directions, but ultimately landed in the same field. A woman, alone and convinced of her imminent demise, wrote her husband a farewell note and nailed it to a rafter. (She lived, and she tore up the note.) Another woman swimming for her life across the bay found herself accompanied by a pack of rats, all desperate to reach dry land. A cow pastured on Moriches Island drifted into a thicket in Benjamintown, almost a mile across the bay.

Patricia Shuttlesworth, whose family arrived every summer from New Jersey with a cook and a chambermaid, recalled emerging from her home a little after 3:00 P.M., thinking that the storm had passed. Actually, the eye was overhead. When the hundred-mile-per-hour winds came up from the southwest shortly after 3:30 and the storm surge slammed their home, they hurried to evacuate. Shuttlesworth's mother crammed her family and guests into a five-passenger Ford, but she could not fit the servants. "She said she would never forget the sight of them standing there, waiting, when the water came up."

The crisis begat such difficult decisions and terrible scenes, colored by class. Yet it also allowed leaders to emerge, regardless of social or economic position. The Countess Charles de Ferry de Fontnouvelle, wife of the French consul general in New York, at first thought that the storm surge at Westhampton Beach was an earthquake. Her beach house was inundated. She bundled up her twenty-three-month-old daughter and they left, along with the governess and the cook. "Water swirled around our hips," she recalled. "Planks, branches, and all sorts of things were flying through the air. It was only by the grace of God that we were not killed." Finally they reached the Ottman home, a half-mile away.

"The hero of everything was the Ottmans' butler," continued the countess. "He quieted everybody when the storm was at its worst." The butler assumed a calm control over the twenty-five refugees. He tried signaling by flashlight, but when help was not forthcoming, he led everyone in linking arms and sloshing to safer ground. They reached the mainland just before the bridge collapsed. The countess stripped down to her undergarments to wade through the whipping waters, and she spent the night at a politician's home. "I wish I knew the name of that brave man," she sighed to reporters, while still in her underclothes. She never asked. His name was Arni Benedictson.

A final story, perhaps apocryphal, captures the surprising power of the hurricane on Westhampton Beach: A man had sent away for a barometer, which he received on September 21. When he saw the needle below 28, he figured it was broken and sent it back with a note of complaint. While he was at the post office, the hurricane blew away his house.

THE OCEAN TORE AN INLET ON THE BORDER between Westhampton Beach and Quogue. Some swore that the channel was four hundred feet wide and twenty feet deep. Much of Quogue was submerged. First the winds tore down trees, chimneys, and even the roof of the Quogue House, the town's largest hotel. Then breakers crashed on front lawns a mile inland. From her second-story window, Helen Rowley Tuthill could see a meadow on lower ground. Sixteen people were clinging to a floating remnant of a building.

Al Peters, who drove a delivery truck for the Quogue Market, had been helping some storm refugees that afternoon when he learned that his house was surrounded by water, with his wife, Mary Jane, and six-year-old daughter, Sally, inside. The water was so deep that Al and two others had to swim down the main streets of Quogue. They passed the Church of Atonement, which had lifted off its foundation and drifted into a small tree grove. On Assop's Neck

An uprooted tree along Main Street, East Hampton (courtesy of the East Hampton Library)

Lane they found an overturned rowboat, righted it, and paddled for the Peters's floating house.

Mary Jane and Sally had spent the afternoon praying. They were soaked from a broken cesspool line, and they were enduring a floating roller-coaster ride as beds, bureaus, radiators, and refrigerators drifted by. Not only did Al rescue them, but the next day, when the village had a temporary food shortage, Mary Jane remembered that just as the storm had started, she had finished cooking pork chops and left them on a high shelf. Although the house was uprooted and mud-soaked, they found the pot intact. The chops were delicious.

The storm surge was nearly as fierce on Southampton Beach. Waves swept two women into Lake Agawam, where they drowned. The waves blasted open the Shinnecock Inlet, which remains today. The hurricane further destroyed all but two Southampton Beach cottages, both of which belonged to an Italian count. Only the east wall of the St. Andrew's Church on the Dunes remained standing, with a verse from Psalms: "Thou rulest the raging of the sea; Thou stillest the waves thereof they arise."

The Bridgehampton freight station shifted onto the railroad tracks. In Sag Harbor, a gust launched the graceful, 125-foot steeple of the Presbyterian Church into the air. The village landmark, which had stood for three generations, smashed to bits. At least there was a heartening note in Riverhead. A healthy Shirley Ann Gatz was born on September 21, 1938, at the Eastern Long Island Hospital at 3:20 P.M., just as part of the hospital's tin roof flew off and flooded the delivery room.

Throughout this rural region, the hurricane had a devastating environmental impact. Salt water rained on the vegetation, browning the leaves that outlasted the storm. Potato farms flooded with seawater. Sand smothered the marshlands, preventing the grasses from growing back. Nearly half the stately elms and locusts that had long arched over the villages, defining their character since colonial times, fell to the storm. Now, *Time* compared the Hamptons to "the Argonne of 1918."

Farthest east on the South Fork, surging waters rendered the fishing villages of Montauk an island. They had no power, no lights, and practically no communication with the outside world for two days afterward. The storm damaged about a hundred buildings. A fisherman named Gene McGovern was in the post office and had to kick out a window to escape just before the first big wave carried the building four hundred yards away.

The hurricane maimed the local fishing industry. Twenty-nine craft blew ashore, some of them three hundred feet up the beach. The schooner *Jean and Joyce* out of Nova Scotia foundered off Sammis Beach, and its seven-man crew fought a tiny dory through the surf onto Old House Landing, where a volunteer rescue crew from East Hampton found them incapacitated by their struggle. The bunker steamer *Ocean View* sank with 125,000 pounds of fish aboard; six of the twenty-three crew members died when their lifeboat capsized. The seventy-nine-year-old painter William Langson Lathrop died after the storm pushed his sailboat to sea.

Yet at sea, just as on land, people survived with some combination of luck and pluck. The four-man crew of the forty-one-foot *Ruth R* had been hauling traps off Culloden Point when the wind picked up. Their trap boats splintered against the side of the sloop, and the gale drove them west toward Gardiners Island. They could not see a boat length ahead, and standing on deck was impossible. They dropped two anchors, but both cables snapped. Water flooded the engine. Then the hurricane swept them north. All night they bailed out the *Ruth R*, their clothes soaked and stomachs empty. Finally they restarted the engine. At 9:00 A.M. on Thursday, they tied up off Block Island. After borrowing some supplies, they returned home. Few of Montauk's old salts hesitated to call it a miracle

❧   ❧   ❧

ON THURSDAY, SEPTEMBER 22, the *New York Times* reporter Pat McGrady accompanied a Coast Guard pilot surveying the damage along the Long Island coastline. The hurricane had destroyed the protective sand dunes, forced back shoreline, and formed eight new inlets, most of which were filled with ruined cars, tree limbs, and the carcasses of homes. They saw piles of kindling where beach villages once stood, perhaps a thousand smashed boats, wrecked cars, fallen trees. "We saw roofs floating without walls, walls without roofs and whole houses afloat."

But they had come to search for the dead. "We saw bodies clad only in shoes and socks," reported McGrady. "The wind had blown off the rest of the clothing." More than fifty people died on Long Island on September 21, 1938. The toll would have been far higher had the hurricane arrived a month earlier, during the peak summer vacation season. On Westhampton Beach, for instance, the summer population of three thousand had shrunk to about eight hundred. But the hurricane was destructive enough. Unfortunately, it was just the first stop on the Long Island Express.

Connecticut

CROSS LONG ISLAND Sound, winds uprooted thousands of trees, rendering much of Connecticut's southwestern coast a forbidding quagmire. Once-stately grounds at Yale University and the New Haven Historical Society looked like war zones. "Here, where the lordliest of trees stood, all is waste and desolation, a scant company left to stand out gaunt and broken, like a lost battalion," eulogized one New Haven man. "This is the crime of the years, the tragedy of generations."

Floodwaters floated an 800,000-gallon oil tank into New Haven harbor, and the winds pushed it up the Quinnipiac River until it nestled against the Ferry Street Bridge. Bridgeport's streets flooded. The roller coasters collapsed at Savin Rock, an amusement resort town off West Haven, and the south side of the main thoroughfare crumbled into the sea. Only concrete septic tanks marked where seaside cottages once stood.

But this region sidestepped the hurricane's full force. The eye bisected Connecticut much as it had Long Island, and the winds west of the eye were weaker. Moreover, because the hurricane spun counterclockwise, the southwestern coast avoided a storm surge. The winds there did not travel along the ocean, so they could not build massive waves, which caused more coastline damage than the winds. So Yale's Gothic structures and Bridgeport's munitions factories easily survived, and New Haven reported only one storm-related death.

Even so, the hurricane was harrowing. In Old Greenwich, near the state's southwest tip, where the storm's effects were mildest, floodwaters forced sixty-one-year-old Henry Weber to spend the night at his neighbor's home. The wind, the water, and the stress so sapped him that he died of a heart attack the next morning.

✿   ✿   ✿

THE SOUTHEASTERN COAST, from Saybrook Point to Stonington, bore the hurricane's full brunt. Here arrived the strongest winds, and the tendrils of Long Island's North and South Forks afforded a flimsy barrier against surging waters.

In Old Saybrook, actress Katharine Hepburn's family had built an elegant summer home on the sandbar forty years earlier. By September 21, most of their neighbors had closed their houses for the season, but Katharine's brother Dick was working on a play and the actress was waiting to hear if she would play Scarlett O'Hara in *Gone with the Wind*. When the hurricane struck, the water rose seventeen feet above mean high water, and waves pounded the bottom floors. Dick led his family and a houseguest through a dining room window, and they marched to higher ground as cars, boats, and sections of neighboring homes flew past. Two chimneys crumbled and the cottage lifted off its foundation, drifting a half-mile away. The next day, the house was a wreck and the family heirlooms were buried in mud, but Dick found his typewriter and files, the former fully functional and the latter bone dry.

At the yachting center of Essex, northeast winds first battered a moored fleet of a hundred sail and power boats. Within three hours, the winds reached eighty miles per hour, and the sea rose six feet, rendering the moorings irrelevant. The ships rammed the shore. Then the eye passed, the winds hit from the southwest, and the storm surge rushed up the river's mouth. Boats that had survived the first onslaught succumbed to the second, including the fleet's largest boat, the eighty-foot *Lascar II*, which was swept up and over a sand pile. The schooner escaped with comparatively little damage, but by that night, much of the fleet lay at the bottom of the river. Two yacht captains were still missing days later.

New London offered the ghastliest scene, a chaotic glimpse of Armageddon. This port—the first major city to endure the hurricane's full fury—suffered the triple tragedy of gale winds, a storm surge, and a wicked fire. In September 1781, a month before the British surrender at Yorktown, the traitorous Benedict

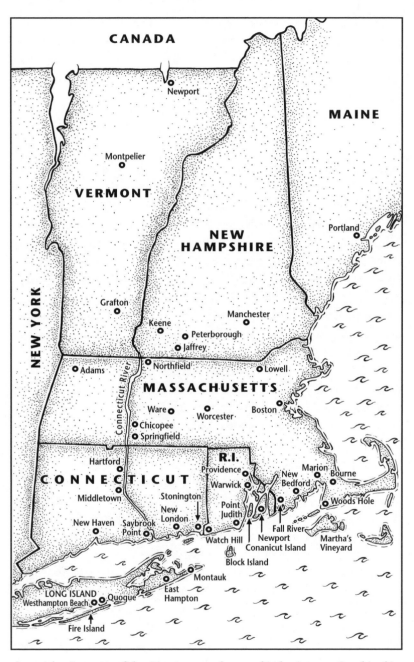

A map showing many of the cities, towns, and geographical points mentioned in this book

*The steamship **Tulip** along the railroad tracks in New London, Connecticut (courtesy of the Connecticut Historical Society)*

Arnold had burned virtually all New London, including its homes and stores, the church and courthouse, its wharves and ships. Only that spiteful scorched-earth campaign rivaled the Hurricane of 1938 for its catastrophic impact upon eastern Connecticut.

When the hurricane arrived around 3:30 in the afternoon, it bucked roofs off buildings, smashed storefront windows, and uprooted trees. Water rushed over the banks of both Long Island Sound and the Thames River, while inland rivers and lakes overflowed into the city. Waves broke downtown. Some ships in port dropped anchor and put their engines on full, but they made no headway into the hundred-miles-per-hour wind. The lighthouse tender *Tulip* heaved onshore behind the Custom House, landing nose first upon the main tracks of the New York, New Haven, and Hartford Railroad. In Ocean Beach, a resort area on the southwest tip of New London's harbor, the storm surge lifted fifty cottages off their foundations, flipping them end over end into a stack of splintery ruins.

On Sparyard Street in the lower harbor, the five-masted barkentine *Marsala* blew out of the water, crossed the railroad tracks, and struck the corner of the

Humphrey-Cornell building, somehow starting a fire. The building was flooded and electric wires short-circuited. At 4:30 a man staggered into the main fire station and reported the conflagration.

For the fire department, it was a worst-case scenario. Firefighters were hacking away at trees to clear roads and answer emergency calls for spot fires throughout the city. Ten minutes after dispatching the first truck to the Humphrey-Cornell building, the department lost all fire alarm communication. Only one telephone line stayed briefly open. By 4:50, chiefs were asking ham operators to radio surrounding towns for help. In New London the firemen had to communicate by foot messengers. Worse, the winds were shooting embers onto warehouses on Starr, Green, and Pearl Streets. The fire was spreading through the entire lower harbor. Trees crisscrossed the surrounding roads, and floodwaters made it impossible to move hose lines. Unable to get their hoses close, the firemen watched the glass windows of the Thompson Garage melt. Water mains snapped, so they tried suctioning tidewater. But it was futile. They could barely stand in the wind, and even the water from their high-pressure hoses dissolved into spray after ten or fifteen feet.

The Coast Guard was the first to provide support, and by 5:30 the Jordan and Oswegatchie fire companies had arrived. But the hurricane was still fervent. The firemen fought a futile battle in near isolation through salty spray and whipping winds, altering their strategy to contain the blaze as the winds shifted direction. Sparks from the burning warehouses flew over to John Street, igniting the New London News Company. Fallen trees kept Engine 6 from reaching the main fire until 6:30, and Engine 7 could not arrive until 8:30, as the winds were abating. At 11:15 another fire started on Pequot Avenue, near Green Harbor Beach, and the Coast Guard helped Engine 5 put it out. Around that time, the fire department considered using dynamite to check the fire's spread. A fortuitous wind shift disabused them of that plan.

The Goshen Fire Department had seen the fire that afternoon, but fallen trees had kept them from New London until 2 A.M. By then the fire had been contained. Thirteen commercial buildings had burned to rubble, and some still smoldered days after the disaster. The fire department's official report counted eighty-nine buildings affected by the hurricane: twenty-five totally destroyed, twenty-one partially destroyed, and forty-three slightly damaged.

The waterfront was a shambles, its boats tossed into the city pier or the railroad station. A fishing fleet tied up in a creek near Trumbull Street was ravaged. Concrete pavement had peeled off the ground. Area hospitals treated fifty-five people. In the earliest reports, two men had drowned, and two others had died in their cars. Ingvald Beaver was trying to tie down part of the barge *Victoria*'s dislodged roof when a massive wave swept him to his death. Alfred Stoll died when struck by an unhinged garage door. That night the Coast Guard, Marines, Navy, and National Guard patrolled the city, stalking shadows of crumbling ruins, flickering in the light of stubborn flames.

∾ ∾ ∾

FOR ALL NEW LONDON'S DEVASTATION, a pilot flying over the region the next day claimed that the area to the east appeared worse off. The coastal villages looked abandoned. Franklin Rathbun of Noank reflected that the hurricane "was without question the most memorable event of my formative years." Then ten years old, he recalled that after lunchtime, his fourth-grade teacher was fighting to speak above howling winds. His father rushed into the schoolroom. "I've come to get my son," the fisherman announced, cutting a startling figure with his stern expression and foul-weather gear, dripping water onto the oiled pine floor. With Franklin's younger brother, they fought through the gale, one step at a time. "Your whole being is immersed in a howling, vibrating universe that imparts an almost nightmarish sensation," described Rathbun. The ground was covered with eddying leaves and scurrying branches, and the elm trees lining Main Street crashed before their eyes. Their mother was out of town, so their father brought them to a friend's house, placed them on the parlor couch, spun the sofa around so it faced the wall, and commanded them to keep their heads down. That way the couch's back would block any flying debris.

A local fishmonger burst in. "The waterfront's all gone," he cried. "My fish market's been washed away and the docks are piled up along the shore. . . . I'm ruined, completely ruined!" He was not the only one. After the wind shifted, Franklin's father went to look for his boat, the *Anna R*, the family's sole source of income. He saw her flowing up the flooded Mystic River.

After the storm died down, the Rathbun boys ate jelly sandwiches while peering out salt-caked windows, spotting little but fallen trees. That evening they surveyed Noank. The church's steeple and roof had blown off, and 90 percent of Main Street's elms had crashed down. On the waterfront, "the air was so full of spume it seemed to be misting." The water was fourteen feet above normal. Six Penny Island was submerged, only the tip of Ram's Island peeked above rolling seas, and huge sheets of foam were breaking on Mason's Island. The Rathbun home on Riverview Avenue remained standing, but the chimney top had crumbled off, the waterfront windows and shingles had caved in, and water soaked everything. Waves were still crashing debris against the house.

Mrs. Orris B. Norman, the postmaster, janitor, and clerk of the village of Old Mystic, rode out the early part of the storm from the post office. But when the winds started rocking the old stone structure, she called her dog, Patsy, and headed for her home next door. She saw a huge elm tree crash down on telephone wires, felling a pole in front of their house. Patsy scooted back into the post office. Mrs. Norman dashed home, and she found her brother frantically trying to protect their house. They nailed a French door into the frame and tried fastening linoleum over the attic windows. "We had to abandon that," she recalled, "when the blinds in the kitchen began to bang and window lights began to shower down like ripe apples." Her crockery smashed, leaving a jagged mess on the kitchen floor.

When a living-room window broke open, the wind almost knocked her out of the house. She found a replacement storm window, which they nailed in after a struggle. The floodwaters kept rising. Mrs. Norman remembered Patsy, and she waded through waist-deep water back to the post office. But she could not find her dog amidst the whirlpool. Through the evening, she and her brother carried salvageable goods upstairs. Another brother arrived home in a rowboat. When her husband came home, he related that a telephone pole had landed on his bus, and he and his passengers had taken shelter in an office building. Drained from the endeavor, Mrs. Norman fainted.

They found Patsy the next day, safe but exhausted from paddling for her life.

THE PASSENGER TRAIN *Bostonian* was carrying 275 passengers, including many students returning to New England prep schools and colleges. The train had departed Grand Central Station at noon, ahead of the storm. When the train rolled into New London soon after 3:00, the hurricane was catching up. Wind and rain assaulted the cars, and passengers pressed their faces against the right-side windows to watch the barkentine *Marsala*, already blown loose and heading for the lower harbor. The train pressed on, following the tracks along Long Island Sound. By the time they reached Mystic, boards and tree branches were flying overhead, and water was creeping onto the tracks. Around 3:30 the train braked just west of Stonington, the easternmost station along the Connecticut coast. The gravel trestle leading into town had flooded over, and the railroad had ordered all its trains to halt.

The engineer and fireman hopped out to investigate. After rounding a bend, they saw a train in front of them and turned back. Then water rushed at them, and they began sprinting. Water rose to their ankles, then their knees, then their waists. When they reached the train, they saw the three rear cars, undercut by waves, leaning toward the sound. They had to evacuate. The passengers started moving toward the engine. Their initial good humor disintegrated into panic as the windward windows cracked and shattered, as salty water and glass shards sprayed them, and as waves pounded the train. One massive green wave sent the bow of a thirty-foot sailboat crashing through a window, leaving the car tilted sideways.

The rear parlor car had been reserved for returning students of the Fessenden School, a prep school in West Newton, Massachusetts. Stuck at the back of the slow-moving chain, some of the boys decided to get off on the leeward side and walk along the trestle. "We looked out," recalled one boy, then twelve years old and leaving home for the first time. "There was nothing but water and wind and a curious smell, almost a burning smell. Water stretched as far as I could see, and scattered houses appeared to float on it. The wind was maniacal. It sounded like unceasing jeering, and it was punctuated with thuds and crashes as debris smashed into the windward side of the train. Everything—homesickness, fear, and chagrin over the prospect of getting my brand-new Rogers Peet clothes *wet*—hit at once, and I started to weep."

Panic reigned. Those walking along the trestle had to negotiate slippery railroad ties buried underneath knee-deep water, and they sank to their necks when they misstepped. The wind funneled between cars knocked many of them into a flooded field. Some swam back, others swam to higher ground. Some people pulled themselves to safety along a line stretched between the train and a tree. Those walking in the train shuffled forward, fearing that the cars would tip over amid escalating waters. Boats and debris kept slamming the windward side. Some jumped into the sound through doors and windows. An elderly Hartford woman jumped into the water and disappeared. When steward Chester Walker tried to swim to a nearby highway, a huge piece of wood struck him in the head, and he drowned, too. Still, the train crew urged calm, ferried passengers forward, grabbed provisions from the dining car, and tried to prevent a descent into anarchy.

The derailed train outside Stonington, Connecticut (courtesy of the Connecticut Historical Society)

About 160 people crammed into the engine and front car. The clamor from stimulated passengers almost drowned out the storm. Time grew precious as the water level rose. The parlor car had already tipped. The brakes were locked. The firebox had cooled, but the conductor had some steam left. A courageous brakeman dove into the water, fought through the undertow and floating debris, and uncoupled the engine and first car from the rest. Three times the engineer tried starting forward. Three times the wheels refused to grip the track. On the fourth try, he opened full throttle. The locomotive yawned, bellowed, and then moved. The passengers cheered.

Crawling across the trestle, the train dragged along uprooted utility poles until the wires snapped. It nudged a cabin cruiser aside. It then poked the side of a house that had washed upon the tracks, and the structure tumbled into the water. It finally ascended into Stonington station, just fifteen minutes before huge waves swept the remaining cars clean of the trestle. The crew of the *Bostonian* had saved many lives.

Stonington itself had been shut off from the world: Every road and street was blocked, electricity and telephones were out, twenty-eight houses on two seaside streets had washed away, and the landmark Community House tower and clock had toppled. Yet its citizens took care of the hurricane's refugees, including those from the *Bostonian.* Those exiting from the right of the train stayed at the parish hall at St. Mary's Church. Those exiting from the left, including the weepy Fessenden boy, stayed at the Town Hall. A kind woman cut off the boy's shrunken necktie before it strangled him. To feed the refugees, town employees raided a marooned delivery truck for soft cheese and canned corned beef, and they requisitioned coffee and sugar from a grocery. Before they fell asleep on makeshift beds of lined-up chairs, the exhausted passengers were entertained by two fellow refugees, vaudeville actors who played the piano, sang, and joked away the nerve-racking day.

"CONNECTICUT STRUGGLED TODAY WITH THE WORST flood conditions since March of 1936," reported the *Hartford Courant*, referring to a major flood that had occurred two years earlier. Water was "pouring off the saturated land throughout the state, swelling brooks, flooding highways, undermining bridges, interrupting train and bus service and bringing mounting damage in its wake." State police were on around-the-clock emergency duty. Damage estimates ran in the hundreds of thousands of dollars. Families were abandoning their homes. There was an ironic shortage of drinking water.

The report was from Wednesday, September 21—the morning *before* the Hurricane of 1938 struck.

New England's weather had been particularly bizarre that summer. Record precipitation fell in June and July, and August had been unusually muggy. The rains returned in September. On both September 12 and September 15, it had rained over an inch, causing high groundwater and river levels. From September 17 through September 20, it had rained constantly, falling heaviest on September 20. In the Thames River basin, thirteen inches of rain fell in five days. Some reported as much as seventeen inches of rain. Flood levels along the Connecticut River neared the highs of March 1936, and there were record flows from its tributaries, such as the Deerfield, Millers, and Chicopee.

These preexisting conditions exacerbated the hurricane's impact. Connecticut had withstood the floods prior to September 21. Since the 1936 flood, cities had built protective dikes and factories had relocated to higher ground. The hurricane added only three inches of rainfall, but powerful winds forced the rivers to carry volumes far beyond their capacity. The most devastated areas beyond coastal New England were thus in the major river basins, which suffered the twin calamities of wind and flood.

The floods also shaped the storm's course and enduring strength. Hurricanes depend upon pulling warm, humid air upward, so they typically peter out while traveling over land. On September 21, however, much of Connecticut was a pool of warm and shallow water, so the storm could travel inland and still feed off moist conditions, as if it continued to move across tropical seas. Also, the eye was traveling atypically fast, at about seventy miles per hour, nearly as fast as the air particles swirling around it. A hurricane dies out in northern climes because cold air sweeps into the center column. But by the time cold air swirled into this storm, the warm inner core had moved another sixty miles. Thus, thanks to the flood conditions and the storm's speed, the Hurricane of 1938 sustained its power while following an unusual inland path through the heart of Connecticut.

The environmental damage was appalling. The state's Park and Forest Commission estimated that the timber industry suffered losses over $1.5 million, that more than a hundred thousand public shade trees fell, and that the number of destroyed private shade and orchard trees was too high to gauge. A police officer in Meriden swore that he saw one huge elm tree uprooted at a forty-five degree angle, only for a wind shift to slam it back upright, as if nothing had happened. Tobacco sheds lifted into the air, lowland areas flooded, and rivers gushed over their banks.

Streets and lawns became rivers and waterfalls. Large sections of Wethersfield and Windsor were submerged, and Cromwell was a lake. Two dams near Rockville broke, and when the larger Snipsic Lake Dam looked about to burst, many fled the town for surrounding hills. In East Hampton, the Bevin Brothers Company dam bulged and popped, though the Civilian Conservation Corps and the town's citizens heroically patched it. Had the dam broken, the town would have been under water. Main Street was still so flooded that three days after the storm, a man caught a seventeen-pound carp in front of a downtown general store.

Charles Dickens had once called High Street in Middletown "the most beautiful street in America," but after the hurricane it was covered by a messy carpet of branches, leaves, and uprooted trunks. The city sat near the swollen Connecticut River, which flooded roads to the east and south. At Wesleyan

Two men climb above a flooded Holland Brook, in South Glastonbury, Connecticut (courtesy of the Connecticut Historical Society)

University, the hurricane struck during the matriculation ceremony. President James McConaughy continued his address even after the chapel's lights went out at 3:10. Most students filed out after singing the Alma Mater at 3:30, but about a hundred people stayed inside. Students peeked out the door, howling with glee. But some professors who had already left could see the wood-beamed steeple swaying. At 4:15 it crashed through the roof, showering down plaster. One observer later compared the experience to an air raid. No one was seriously hurt, though one panicked professor did dive under a pew.

Churches across the state shared the fate of Wesleyan's chapel. The towering, courtly steeple of the Westfield Congregational Church, perched upon the large town green in Danielson, leaned, rocked, and then fell before the front entrance. The newly renovated St. James Church in Manchester lost its steeple, which tore large chunks off the south wall. The reservoir in Glastonbury had already given way on September 20. On September 21, the storm not only crushed factories, homes, and three radio towers, but also blew out the walls of the First Congregational Church. Its steeple plunged into the debris.

A flooded neighborhood in Hartford, Connecticut (courtesy of the Connecticut Historical Society)

The hurricane hit Hartford around 4:00. Snapped branches and massive trunks soon littered the once-pristine grounds of the State Capitol. Traffic ground to a halt: Tree trunks blocked roads, pavement shattered to pieces, and soaked car engines stalled. Much of the city lost electricity. Streets were littered with shards of glass, the remnants of peeled-off roofs, and bricks from crumbling buildings. Winds carried off a Vine Street veranda.

But even as the winds slackened, the Connecticut River rose at a rate of four inches an hour. By midnight, the river reached over twenty-four feet high, and it kept rising until noon the next day. The heart of the nation's insurance capital was flooded. (Ironically, the city carried very little flood insurance.) Commerce Street, Front Street, and the lower end of State Street were submerged. By the next morning, the flood had spread to the north end of Main Street and the Windsor Street underpass. Police and National Guardsmen patrolled downtown Hartford in boats. While maneuvering past floating cars, they saw rats and rabbits frantically paddling for high ground. More than seven thousand people had to abandon their homes in the Connecticut River's floodplains, including all those in the western part of East Hartford.

During the twenty-four hours after the hurricane struck, twelve hundred workers—government laborers, World War I veterans, college students, and other volunteers—built a levee that saved the southeast section of Hartford, a district of five thousand homes and numerous industries. From the dikes near Colt's Patent Fire Arms, they packed sandbags, targeting weak spots where streams leaked through. The Connecticut River had risen more than thirty-three feet. The workers' effort seemed a model of quiet determination, broken only by the occasional bark of a foreman or the rumble of another truck delivering sandbags. At points the river reached within inches of the makeshift rampart, and not until 10:00 P.M. on September 23 did the water start to recede. But the levee held, and the neighborhood survived.

❧ ❧ ❧

IN CONNECTICUT, ON SEPTEMBER 21, the Angel of Death arrived in many guises. George Kirby of Westport was picking up branches in his yard when a tree fell on him. Charles Krolikowsky of Stratford was struck by his own dislodged roof. In Branford, a tree crushed the car of Mrs. Carl Carlson as she sat in traffic. Harry Warshauer, an employee at a Willimantic factory for just one week, was killed when a dislodged section of the building fell on him. Patrick Jones of Cheshire slammed against a building with such violence that he suffered fatal head and chest injuries. In Naugatuck, fallen power lines electrocuted John Daly of the State Highway Department. Mary Kenifick of Hartford had a heart attack. A tree landed on John Chessey of Tolland, and it took three hours to get him the five miles to the nearest hospital, where he died two hours later. In Stamford, a gate blew open and threw back George Hoyt, fracturing his skull.

On September 23, the *Hartford Courant* reported fifty-four people dead and twenty missing. Estimates of property damage rose into the millions of dollars. The hurricane had wounded major cities and tiny hamlets, yachting havens and fishing villages, textile mills and tobacco farms. It had spared neither the poor nor the wealthy. Yet it had compelled extraordinary struggles by people such as the firemen of New London, the crew of the *Bostonian*, and the squad that saved the Colt's dike. The hurricane may have flaunted nature's power, but it also gave man a chance to shape his own destiny.

CHAPTER FOUR

Rhode Island

"OH MY GOD, I am heartily sorry," prayed ten-year-old Anne Moore.

"Oh my God, I am heartily sorry," repeated her four-year-old sister, Margaret.

"For having offended Thee."

"For having offended Thee."

From the attic of the family cottage at Watch Hill, they continued through the Act of Contrition. Waves were breaking over their roof, and the bottom floors had collapsed beneath them. Lumps of concrete from the seawall walloped what remained of the sprawling, three-story barn structure. The storm had already claimed the other homes in their Fort Road neighborhood, and when the Moores had tried to escape by car, the garage door would not open. So all eleven people in the Moore household—Anne and Margaret, their mother and father, their brother and sister, a family friend, three servants, and their neighbor—retreated to the attic. Unsure whether they could save their lives, the girls sought to save their souls.

The Moore cottage was anchored in concrete and protected by a bulky seawall on its ocean side. Sitting between the magnificent Atlantic and picturesque Little Narragansett Bay, they often called it "Heaven on Earth." On

September 21, it seemed closer to hell. Mr. Moore had suffered a heart attack that morning, and his doctor had confined him to bed rest. Moore had instead barricaded windows and comforted his children as the storm rendered his home the last bastion of civilization along Fort Road. It would not stand much longer.

Two days later, the *Providence Bulletin* reported that the cottage had been swept away and the Moores had disappeared. But in fact, as the girls prayed, the wind ripped off part of the roof, and it flipped over onto the sea. The family climbed into the makeshift raft, huddling together and grabbing onto the two pipes attached to its floor. One wall jutted upward and acted as a sail. Gargantuan waves crashed upon them and hammerhead sharks followed them like vultures. The raft floated clear across the peninsula, washed into the bay, and finally drifted into a cove on Barn Island. There the Moores found an abandoned barn and spent the night clustered on the leeward side of a haystack, the reflections of the New London fire providing an eerie night-light. A lobsterman rescued them the next morning.

The Moores and their servants were lucky. From Watch Hill to Napatree Point, a thin, natural barrier beach divided the ocean from bays and salt ponds. "If you build on a barrier beach, you are toying with Nature," mused the writer R. A. Scotti. "It is borrowed land on loan from the sea, and eventually, inevitably, the sea will come back to claim it." All thirty-nine houses in that stretch of dunes succumbed to the hurricane, and forty-two people were launched into the bay. Besides the Moore contingent, only five others survived. The only man-made structures to endure on the peninsula were embattlements from the Spanish-American War, where a young couple and two clammers took refuge. (The couple married the next year, figuring that if they could survive the hurricane, they could weather any hardship together.)

Watch Hill epitomized the vulnerability of South County, Rhode Island. Open to the storm surges building up from the Atlantic, vulnerable to the strongest winds east of the eye, and dotted with villages of beach cottages, the twenty-mile stretch from Napatree Point to Point Judith paid the hurricane's stiffest toll: entire communities destroyed, and 175 people lost.

Waves carved a pair of massive inlets at Sandy Point and reduced the once-unbroken coastline of Napatree Point into a series of tiny islands. When the storm surge hit the Watch Hill Yacht Club, according to one witness, the structure cracked in two, and a piano flew out "like a big black bird." The Coast Guard tower on Watch Hill swayed in winds up to 150 miles per hour, and waters enveloped the glacial rock at its foundation, stranding the officers inside. Off Point Judith, the tugboat *May* turned upside down and then flipped right side up again.

"It was like a dike had burst," recalled Frederick Buffum, proprietor of the Weekapaug Inn. He remembered the Atlantic, the beach, and Quonochontaug Pond covered in frothing white water. The storm had also cut two deep channels, leaving the inn on its own island. Buffum had just closed his business for the season, and his staff tried to save the place by nailing a table over shattered dining-room windows. But the entire west wing broke off, and a cottage drifted away. Its second story landed intact on the north shore of the pond—its beds still made, its pictures and mirrors still hanging on the walls.

Elsewhere along the coast, entire villages collapsed into the sea. The community near Napatree Point simply ceased to exist. Sixty cottages at Misquamicut Beach were completely submerged, and only six of two hundred homes remained standing. Charlestown Beach was stripped clean of human habitation. The wind shot chimney bricks hundreds of feet, and the storm surge carried away every shard of wood. More than fifty bodies were found that night, washed up in the dunes.

On Block Island, ten miles south of Point Judith, the hurricane decimated the local economy of fishing, farming, and tourism. All but fourteen of a hundred-boat fishing fleet were lost. At the main harbor, at the mouth of the breakwater, more than a dozen boats piled on top of each other. Other craft washed up miles inland. Sea captain Frank Holwell was blown off his boat; he was last seen hugging his topmast for dear life. The relatively treeless landscape meant that winds tossed about livestock and ripped apart every barn on Block Island. (Much of the farmland was soon overgrown with bayberry, which remains today). The winds also ravaged the hotels, with particularly tragic consequences for William Fuller, who died when a tin roof flew off a hotel and struck his neck.

"I saw summer playgrounds of rich and workingman alike turned into debris, and heard the cries of friends and neighbors struggling on the rooftops of homes swept to sea," reported William Cawley of Westerly, two days after the tragedy. "Some I later counted among the rows of dead. Others I never expect to see alive again." He watched Alvin Mawley, one of his best friends, dive into angry waters to rescue his drowning wife. Husband and wife both died.

The efforts to save loved ones resulted in some of the grimmest imaginable tragedies. Ralph Bliven of Misquamicut saved his eight-month-old daughter by

One of the few houses still standing on Misquamicut Beach in South County, Rhode Island (courtesy of the Providence Public Library)

holding her above water while grasping a heavy floating log, but he saw his wife and sister drown. On Charlestown Beach, as Katherine Burchill's cottage washed into Salt Water Pond, she grabbed her four-year-old daughter. But the girl's dress tore off, and Mrs. Burchill lost her grip and her child. Also on Charlestown Beach, Timothy Mee's wife and two children hurtled out of his arms when the storm surge hit; he landed alone on the shore of Green Hill Pond, and he spent the next few days refusing to leave the morgue, looking for his family's bodies, and finding only the corpse of his baby, Jean.

As the sea washed through Galilee, fourteen-year-old Blake Hareter waded through the streets, holding his mother in one hand and his dog in the other. His mother fell, and he pulled her up. She pleaded with him to drop the dog and save himself. "No, mother, no!" he insisted. Blake's father found them taking refuge under a porch. But a piece of wreckage fell on Blake, killing him instantly. The nightmare continued as surging waters washed the dead boy out of his father's arms, and Mrs. Hareter floated away from her husband. The heartsick pair reunited hours later at the South County Hospital in Wakefield.

The extraordinary circumstances also compelled extraordinary heroism. In Weekapaug, a Red Cross lifeguard named Henry Morris swam across a raging breachway with a rope, then escorted five stranded vacationers across the channel. For that feat he earned the Carnegie Medal of Heroism. In Galilee, five people took refuge on the roof of a flooded home, where wind and water assaulted them for two hours. Finally the waves undercut the house, and it floated for a half-mile, coming to a rest near the State Pier. They rightfully feared getting blown into the water and drowning. But James Gamache had been riding out the storm from his thirty-five-foot dragger, tied to the now-submerged pier. He dove into the water, pulling his dory alongside him. The storm had rendered his oars useless, yet Gamache swam through a hurricane while attached to a rowboat. Then he towed back the dory—with all five people in it! His remarkable courage saved them. They all spent the evening aboard the tugboat *May*, which had made for a safe harbor after getting flipped by the waves.

For others, too, survival depended on some fusion of fate and fortitude. Helen Joy Lee remembered emerging from her Fort Road cottage as the eye passed over: "The sea was flat except for the rollers, the white froth looked as if it was being stirred into a green cake mixture." Her cottage had weathered the early storm, but around 4:00 P.M., the one-hundred-mile-per-hour winds started lashing in from the southeast. Sandy spray seeped under the door, and part of the roof flew off. In minutes she was ankle-deep in water. She went to the side porch, figuring that she could escape if the house collapsed. The glass door smashed in and the shards struck her back. A huge wave knocked her down. Her kitten, stored in her overcoat pocket, "sailed away like a miniature rug."

For a half-hour, she felt her house shake with every wave, and projectiles of debris flew past her. Then a wave crushed the porch, dislocating Helen's elbow and shooting her 150 feet away. She dove underneath a potentially decapitating piece of wood and then swam through deep water to grab onto a pole. She could barely see through the spray, gray with sand. When she climbed onto the floating side of a house, a flying bookshelf smacked her in the eye. Trying to drift out of this danger zone, she kept switching vessels— first to a mattress, then to a boat. At 6:30, her boat scratched the tops of twenty-foot trees. Around 8:00, the winds subsided, and she climbed down onto a tree. She made a pillow out of roof shingles and a blanket out of dune grass, and she periodically dozed. She had floated across the bay into Connecticut.

At 4:00 A.M. Helen started walking by the light of the stars, fighting over wreckage with her one good arm. She fell into ditches three times. Around

6:30 she found a helpful family. An "Uncle Fred" offered to take her to Westerly Hospital, but first they had to hike a half-mile to a car, and then drive six miles over bumpy fields to get past fallen trees. At 8:15 they arrived at the hospital. Helen had a broken arm, two black eyes, a swollen jaw and nose, scratches covering her legs and arms, feet pricked with thorns, and an inch-long stick of wood jammed into the bridge of her nose.

A friend who worked at the hospital heard her voice. "Is that Mrs. Lee?" she called out.

"Yes," Helen replied. "What's left of her."

◊ ◊ ◊

"MY BABY'S JUST BEEN BLOWN OUT OF MY ARMS!" yelled a frantic woman rushing into The Outlet department store. The wind had started shooting hats off people's heads, and storefront windows were rattling and bulging. A beat cop saved the woman's "baby"—he arrived a few minutes later toting a disheveled two-year-old boy—but the hurricane was coming to Providence.

After 4:00 P.M., a chunk of the Providence Public Library's roof tore off. Soon afterward, the steeple of St. Patrick's Church, located behind the State House, crashed down and onto the church roof. The arch above Union Station started crumbling, ripping off the metal roof "with a roar like a boiler factory," according to author Van Wyck Mason, who had just arrived in the city. Glass rained upon would-be commuters.

Streetlights were popping like firecrackers. The city's tall buildings and narrow streets formed nasty wind tunnels. As one group ran from the Arcade to better-protected grounds, a shattered plate-glass window crashed down on them, slicing an elderly woman in the neck. They ran into a crowded lobby, all spattered with blood, the old woman soaked in it. "It was at that point that our senses wouldn't go on," remembered one man. "They only registered latently and feebly what we saw and heard."

The winds were just a precursor to Providence's true catastrophe. Thanks to the Weather Bureau's mismanagement, the city had received its earliest hurricane warning at 3:40 P.M. By then, the storm had already arrived. Worse, no one predicted the scale of annihilation. Thanks to an unfortunate cocktail of urban layout, hurricane weather, and Rhode Island geography, a massive flood smote Providence.

Much of downtown lay on low ground by the water's edge. During its industrial expansion in the late nineteenth and early twentieth centuries, the city had built up along the Providence River, and its business district was laid in a foundation of wet clay. Flooded basements were common, and four days of rain before September 21 had raised groundwater levels. Also, Providence stands at the top of Narragansett Bay, which narrows to its northern tip. The hurricane's strongest winds blew water up the tapering bay, funneling the water into a larger and larger wave. Compounding the effect, the surge hit at high tide. The Providence River rose over seventeen feet above mean low water.

As the wall of water rushed up Narragansett Bay, it crushed acres of coastline into the sea. It tore through Warwick, destroying over a hundred homes at Conimicut Point and leaving about one hundred people homeless at Oakland Beach. (The victims included a vacationing Woonsocket couple, their maid, their two-year-old son, and their six-month-old daughter. A huge wave overturned their automobile.) It also caused a huge gas tank in East Providence to explode, sending a reverberation felt for miles around.

The surge first hit Providence three miles south of downtown at Field's Point. It inundated the waterfront's oil and coal plants, and it lifted cars off the ground. The waves swept through a lumberyard and deposited the debris in the web of the Point Street Bridge. As the surge kept moving north, barges heaved out of the harbor and careened into Fox Point Square.

Meanwhile, water was spurting out of manholes in downtown Providence. At 5:00, a clerk from the F. A. Ballou shoe store called the offices of the *Providence Journal* and asked when the water would go down. The reporter had no idea what she meant. "The water in the street," she said. "It's flooding the store." It had reached the level of the sidewalk.

The storm surge struck downtown around 5:15, just as electric power failed and many workers were spilling out of their offices. A white wall of water, covering Dyer Street to the west and South Water Street to the east, rushed up the Providence River. A couple standing near the Crawford Street Bridge got swept away and slung around a corner onto Custom House Street. The water gushed west across downtown—"almost as fast as if you held a glass in front of a spigot," according to Solomon Brandt, a Weybosset Street printer. Providence's narrow and curved streets, packed-in buildings, and sea-level business district created perfect conditions for a downtown flood.

The ensuing hours were surreal. No one had anticipated a hurricane, let alone some watery apocalypse. Within minutes, seawater roiling with white-

Oakland Beach in Warwick, Rhode Island (courtesy of the Providence Public Library)

caps swept through the city streets, rising as high as thirteen feet. Van Wyck Mason saw a woman wading to high ground "when she popped out of sight like a jack-in-the-box. She evidently stepped into an open sewer." The water reached the tips of street signs in Market Square, and Exchange Place was a graveyard of floating automobiles and inundated trolley cars. "It was like you put water in a pan," marveled Armand DiMartino, who watched the scene from the top-floor ballroom of the Biltmore Hotel. "It just swirled right in just like something was pushing it in there."

Downtown Providence now hosted a ludicrous floating parade. The floodwaters sent refrigerators bobbing up a department store's basement stairs and onto Weybosset Street. They joined a flotilla of other appliances, cars, boats, barrels, footballs, dolls, tree branches, furniture, clothes, tires, and entire store counters with goods still on top—not to mention people, some stripped to their underwear and others just naked. "It was a token that the urban world had been overthrown and chaos reigned," the *Providence Journal* would reflect. There were some light touches. A big gray rat, perched atop a gasoline tin, floated down Westminster Street. A man stood in knee-deep water downstream from a haberdashery, trying on floating hats until he found a perfect fit.

But mostly, a sense of chaos mixed with fear and disbelief. "No amount of repetitious description could possibly picture what the mind at first failed to grasp completely," reported the *Providence Bulletin*. "A downtown Providence under raging water, men diving from high signs on the sides of buildings, men swimming for their lives on Westminster Street and Exchange Place, all to the tune of a screaming wind that tore with vicious fingers at tall buildings and shook this city to its very foundations." Some cars' headlights still worked, and they shined an eerie underwater glow. But car horns shorted out, and they bleated throughout the ordeal. Harrowing near-death experiences suddenly became commonplace. At Pierce's Shoe Store, the clerk and his customer climbed up a ladder as water rushed in. They waited out the flood from the top of the ladder, with just one foot of air between the water and the high ceiling.

Surviving the flood often depended on heroics and cooperation. On Transit Street, the bartender Harold Quinn dove into the water and pulled a fire hose across the street to the Texaco gas station, saving two stranded men who could not swim. On Dorrance Street, two policemen and four drugstore clerks linked arms against the tide, anchoring the escape of twenty-four people from a shoe store. On Westminster Street, another human chain broke three times as a hysterical woman kept losing her grip. But the others stayed patient, grimly determined, and they eventually pulled her to safety. Elsewhere, four men and a woman swam out of a flooded restaurant and pulled themselves up a rope lowered by a janitor on the second story of the Tribune Building.

But the crisis could also spark contradictory impulses in people. Teenagers Flora Magnan and Helen Harrington were in Thompson's Restaurant on Westminster Street when water bubbled through the floor, up to their waists. The customers climbed onto tables. "That's when the rosary beads came out and the prayers started," recalled Flora, fearing death. As the water kept rising and the tables started floating, some men broke the door to the cafeteria's second-floor bakery, and they guided the women and children up the stairs. Flora remembered one panicky man clambering past them, and the men in charge tossing him away and chiding him. Helen painted a more chaotic picture, with many more men pushing and yelling up the stairs.

Whatever the truth, everyone made it upstairs. The kitchen was cramped and an oven had sprung a gas leak, however, so they climbed another flight via the fire escape. One woman had broken both legs after the wind tossed her against a brick wall; she screamed in agony as the men lifted her. While in the kitchen, Flora had placed a pie in her schoolbag. As they waited out the flood from the third floor, the girls offered pie to their fellow refugees, and some accepted, scooping it out with their fingers. Compassion and composure, spinelessness and selfishness—all were on display during the hurricane.

So was tragedy. Nine people died in Providence, including three women—Clorinda Lupoli, Hilda Pieczentkowski, and Dorothy Atwood—who died in three separate accidents when roofs or chimneys fell on their automobiles. In scenes that would have seemed unfathomable an hour earlier, James McDuff got trapped under a car on Westminster Street, and Chester Hayes was swept by floodwaters into Exchange Place; both men drowned on the streets of downtown Providence.

Commuters had rushed into the second stories of public buildings—fire stations, department stores, even City Hall. Five hundred people took shelter in the Narragansett Hotel, and hundreds more at the Biltmore. People of all faiths sought peace in the Grace Episcopal Church, their only light the flutter of altar candles. Thousands spent the evening in public buildings, and hundreds stayed the night. Van Wyck Mason, whom the *New York Times* would later report missing, actually stayed at the all-male Hope Club. That night, for the first time ever, women passed through the club's doors. Of course, they were hurricane refugees. "The oldsters didn't like it," wrote Mason. "They said no good would come of it."

Joe Fogel and Lorraine Martin had arranged their wedding for the night of September 21 on the second-floor ballroom of the Narragansett Hotel. But while the Martin family waited, the flood kept the Fogels stuck at Union Station. "We were nervous. The hours went by," recalled Lorraine. "Where is he? Where is everybody? What's happened? And there was no way to find out." Meanwhile, the storm's refugees ate their wedding feast and drank their nuptial champagne. Finally Joe arrived around 11:00 P.M. Presided over by a hurrying minister anxious to find his own family, Joe and Lorraine got married by candlelight.

Walking to their honeymoon suite at the Biltmore, the newlyweds may have been the only ones in Providence oblivious to the devastation. The water had receded almost as quickly as it had rushed in. By 10:00 the streets stunk

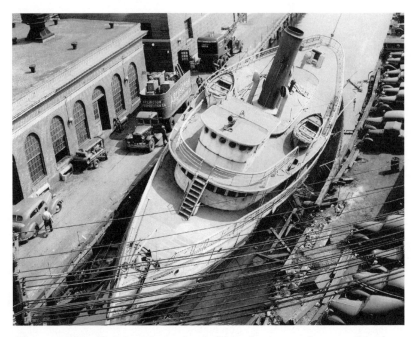

*The steamer **Monhegan**, sunken and wedged into the pier near downtown Providence (courtesy of the Boston Public Library)*

with mud, and they were filled with ruined cars and crumbled bricks. Car horns continued to bleat. The business district was a shambles. Thousands were homeless, electricity was out, and almost all telephones were disconnected. There was no bus, train, or plane service. The next day's *Providence Bulletin* admitted that it could not yet estimate the total damage. It only knew that the Hurricane of 1938 "was and is the greatest disaster that has ever befallen this State."

THE *BULLETIN* ADDED THAT "for all the people of Providence knew, all Europe might have been aflame with war, and Newport, Block Island, and Bristol might as well have been in the middle of the African jungle for communication purposes." Not only were telephones, telegraphs, and transportation services crippled, but each community had its own consuming struggles on September 21, its own unique experiences with the hurricane.

***Destruction along Narragansett Bay, in Conimicut, Rhode Island (courtesy of the
Boston Public Library)***

The region north of Providence dodged the flooding that befell the capital, but not the bruising wind and rain. In Pawtucket, Daniel Jones had just reported for work on the top floor of the Trades Building when he saw the steeple of the First Congregational Church pitch onto Broadway. Minutes later the chimney of his own building crashed through his ceiling and ripped out his floor, damaging the Perfect Silk Company one floor below. Jones somehow survived. Pawtucket's sole casualty was the septuagenarian Philias Bergeron, who rushed home at the height of the storm and then collapsed in his own hallway. According to his doctor, the hurricane literally "took his breath away."

In Woonsocket, John Callanan, father of a priest and four schoolteachers, died when his chimney fell through his roof, burying him in his own kitchen. On Main Street and in Flynn Square, people sought refuge in store entrances as plate-glass windows wobbled, bulged, and then burst onto the street. As the winds diminished, some youths staged an impromptu fashion show, flourishing wind-tossed ladies' hats and dresses.

On the east side of Narragansett Bay, eleven-foot-high storm tides and hundred-mile-per-hour winds left a wake of boats, cars, and splintered houses in gruesome stacks. At least fourteen people died in Barrington, where the storm knocked out the railroad bridge over Narrow River, leaving tracks jutting oddly upward, "like a picket fence." Wind and water reduced the community of Bay Springs into an unrecognizable pile of splinters. Barrington also lost the steeple of its Congregational Church, and only the Kleistone Rubber Company saw a silver lining: "The beautiful old spire will have to be rebuilt, the great bell will have to be rehung, the entire structure will have to be inspected and much of it reconditioned," wrote the company's promoters. "But the Kleistone Rubber tile floor came through storm and flood, slime, salt and mud—*as good as new*."

A huge oyster boat in Warren ripped off its moorings and rode three hundred feet into the center of town, while seven or eight homes in East Warren washed into the sea. The flood in Bristol wedged a gas tank between two houses, and the wind ripped off the steeple of the Methodist Church, sending its thousand-pound bell somersaulting into the church auditorium. Racing yachts—including *Resolute*, the 1920 America's Cup defender—were destroyed, and one rowboat was launched onto the bar of a saloon.

At a typically busy intersection in Tiverton, only the statue of a single soldier patrolled above the whitecaps. One man abandoned his car on a flooded street, then watched a big wave wash away five passengers in a Packard. He sought refuge on a rooftop with five others. The flood pushed the house into the Sakonnet River, ripped off the walls, and deposited the roof in a grove of trees, where they awaited rescue.

Nineteen people died at Island Park, where the hurricane destroyed all but two of two hundred cottages. Most of the debris washed into a peach orchard one mile away. At one waterfront cottage, an elderly man named George Rodgers urged that his wife board a small and crowded rescue raft. He would wait on the disintegrating porch until the rescuers returned. He survived, she drowned.

Newport, the famed playground of the wealthy at the mouth of Narragansett Bay, endured severe devastation. The Cliff Walk, the long stretches of seawall, the manicured grounds of elite seaside estates—the hurricane shredded them all into masses of muddy, sandy, grass-strewn concrete. Dozens of yachts washed onto land, and the surge propelled a sunken tugboat off the ocean floor and onto the middle of a street. The only structure left standing on Bailey's Beach was the massive bathing pavilion, its wings ripped off and washed away, its center uprooted and perched astride Ocean Drive. "Bailey's Beach All But Vanishes," stated one incredulous headline.

Along the waterfront, in the heart of Newport, one witness described "sirens screeching through the din, signs clanging along the sidewalks, the horns of five hundred submerged automobiles on the Government Landing blowing, and the rain pelting down in torrents." Most bizarre, the pounding waves emancipated thousands of lobsters from their traps. Thames Street was the flooded host to a parade of crustaceans.

来 来 来

BECAUSE SO MUCH OF RHODE ISLAND BORDERS WATER—it seemingly hugs Narragansett Bay—the Hurricane of 1938 crippled the tiny, quirky state as no other. Within two days the authorities gained some sense of the death toll. In the Westerly area, fifty-six were dead and forty-three missing. Eight died in Providence, three in East Providence, ten at Quonset Point, eight in Warwick (with another eight missing), fourteen in Barrington, four dead (and four missing) in Sakonnet, and six in Newport. For the entire state, 226 were known dead, and eighty-two were still missing. Those numbers escalated: Later estimates placed the total dead at anywhere from three hundred to four hundred. The figures may or may not account for the hurricane's other casualties: the weakened elderly who perished soon afterward, the parents irretrievably broken by the loss of their children, the man who fell two stories to his death when he forgot that his back stairs had washed away.

For pure pathos, no hurricane story matches that of Norman Caswell and the eight children on his school bus: twelve-year-old Clayton Chellis and his seven-year-old sister, Marion; five-year-old Constantine Gianitis and his four-year-old brother, John; and the four Matoes children—Joseph Jr., thirteen; Teresa, twelve; Dorothy, eleven; and Eunice, seven. Caswell was driving them home from Thomas H. Clark Elementary School in Jamestown, on Conanicut Island, at the mouth of Narragansett Bay.

Joseph Matoes Sr. had tried to intercept the bus at Mackerel Cove, where waves had already smashed the bathing pavilion, carried away three cars (including his own), and drowned a mother and son. He was on high ground atop a stone wall, hunched down against the wind-driven rain. As the bus rounded the bend and came into sight, Matoes tried to wave Caswell back.

It was too late. Caswell drove the bus through knee-deep water. Halfway across the cove, the bus stalled, and a wave knocked it onto a tilt. Caswell realized that if they stayed on the bus, they would drown. He groped his way behind the bus, opened the rear door, and instructed the children to link arms. The Gianitis boys held each other tight. Arrivals from Greece only weeks before, they spoke no English and looked bewildered. Caswell put a boy in each arm.

Clayton Chellis stood at the front of their human chain. "Clayton, don't let the water get in your eyes," said his sister, Marion—her last words. They opened the bus door. Then a huge wave swept over them. The chain broke in the middle, among the small children. From the distant stone wall, in a momentary glimpse through the whipping salty spray, Matoes Sr. thought he saw two of his girls screaming from atop the bus. Then the ocean washed them all away. Clayton Chellis lost the grip on his sister, but he was such a good swimmer that he survived. No other children did. Joseph Matoes Jr. might have made it, but he drowned while helping his sisters.

The elder Matoes had seen his four children driven away by the onrush of water, and he was helpless to stop it. When the waves passed, he recalled, "I saw something coming through the water, something moving and stretched out." He stumbled to the bus, the wind twice knocking him down. Finally he found a body and kicked it awake: Norman Caswell.

"Please let me die," begged the bus driver. "I lost a whole bunch of kids I had in the school bus. Everything's gone. Please don't move me. Let me die." But Matoes stoically carried Caswell to high ground. They never found his children's bodies. Two days later, someone spotted a white blouse and red skirt floating at sea. They were the clothes Dorothy Matoes was wearing on September 21.

Norman Caswell soon died a broken man. "I got your boy," he had to tell Mr. and Mrs. Chellis, "but your daughter's dead—gone." Mr. Chellis just marched down to the bus and fired rocks through the bus windows. Mr. and Mrs. Gianitis left Conanicut Island the next day. They took none of their possessions, and they never returned.

Clayton Chellis emerged with his spirit intact. He believed that God had blessed him, and he determined to make something of his life. He joined the U.S. Navy in 1944, and he served in the Pacific theater of World War II aboard the USS *Tarawa*. At the end of his commission, just before returning home, he celebrated with his fellow sailors on the beach at Saipan. Emboldened by drink, he swam out beyond the reefs. An excellent swimmer, a man who had never spent any of his nineteen years far from water, the sole child survivor of the Mackerel Cove bus tragedy, Clayton Chellis drowned.

"It makes you cry," recalled an old neighbor. "But God was after him, somehow or other, right?"

CHAPTER FIVE

Massachusetts and Beyond

THE STORM SURGE struck the Massachusetts coast from Horseneck Beach to Buzzards Bay. Richard Hawes of Westport Harbor recalled "this solid black wall of water, which looked like an unusually large roller, coming in to the shore with its top being blown off so that it did not curl up and break like an ordinary wave." He had sent his wife and children home at 4:45 P.M., but he had stayed at the beach out of curiosity. He was not scared, even as he lay on the ground, as shingles flew past him, and as the roof of a bathing pavilion flew off. But at 5:00, the first wave appeared "as a long black band approaching in a world otherwise all gray mist, and it was the one moment of the storm which startled me." For the next few minutes he remembered little besides the confusing violence, the fire-hose blast of water, and the eerie shriek of the wind.

On Horseneck Beach, thirty-foot-high waves crashed over the rock-pile embankment, washing hundreds of large, handsome cottages a quarter-mile inland into an open meadow. The beach itself shrank, pounded into a thinner strip. The St. Rose of Lima Chapel was razed. West Beach and Little Beach were piles of rubble; East Beach was a complete mud flat. The waves undercut all the multistory homes, sweeping them off the beach and killing fourteen people.

After twenty idyllic summers at Horseneck Beach, James Blakney barely fathomed the hurricane's destruction. At the storm's height, he was helping a man get his mother and son to a safer cottage, one across a road covered in waist-deep water. The surging current drove the woman and boy out of their arms, and Blakney never saw the three again. He did get his own wife across, however, and he pried open the cottage door with the screwdriver in his pocket. Then the house ripped off its foundation. When the chimney began buckling, they ran to another cottage. That house, too, started floating away. For about a mile, they drifted through ten-foot-deep white water. They jumped from roof to roof of other floating cottages, including their own home. Finally they landed in a cove and pulled themselves through a thicket of brambles to dry land. Their summer sanctuary had washed into oblivion, but they had survived.

In the working-class coastal town of Ocean Grove, near Fall River, unemployed textile workers had stayed in their summer shacks into late September. Waves now smashed their rickety structures, and the winds plucked off their roofs. It was a crushing blow to those suffering the worst from the Great Depression.

The next day's *Fall River Herald-News* estimated that forty-one people had died in greater Fall River. Many more were missing. Three thousand fallen trees and poles obstructed street traffic, and live wires sparked fires on the roadways. Though no one died within the city limits, the tides inundated the waterfront district, washing over the cobblestone piers and spilling into downtown. The influx stranded some people on the upper floors of the freight house on the Fall River Line pier, where they waited until rescue workers arrived via canoe. Desks and cabinets from waterfront offices floated down the piers, gathering into unsightly agglomerations. In the business district, one-hundred-mile-per-hour winds ripped off a section of the City Hall roof, toppled the Unitarian Church steeple, sent chimneys and roofs to the streets, and silenced Fall River's sole radio station. Shattered display windows scarred Main Street—in one case leaving a single mannequin, stripped nude by the wind.

In Fall River's harbor, the barge *Jess B. Shaw* was torn from its moorings, hurled against the Brightman Street Bridge, and then blown toward the Slades Ferry Bridge, where it sank. Two sailors were stranded on the *Arthur C. Staples* amid raging waters; the fire department rescued them before the boat drifted onto Staples Wharf, got swept back into the harbor, and finally reached dry land near a waterfront garage. Captain Joseph O'Connell survived after diving off his excursion boat *Crystal Wave*, which beached alongside a Somerset home.

Many storm-tossed craft floated north to Somerset, another city with a wrecked waterfront. Most dramatically, the gigantic oil tanker *Phoenix* ripped away from its dock, discharged its cargo, and blew across the river toward the home of Selectman Adam Gifford. The anchor chain tore Gifford's garage off the foundation, and the tanker settled on his front lawn, its stern perched high above Riverside Avenue.

The hurricane crippled nearby New Bedford, a city of textile mills and fishing boats. The Acushnet River rose more than eleven feet above mean high water. Nine cotton factories had to suspend operations; floodwaters ruined their stock and damaged their machinery. More than ten thousand workers lost wages. Winds and waves battered the fishing fleets, and some fishermen spent the storm at sea. The next day many were still missing. "Women stood with babies in their arms and watched the horizon in the ageless manner of wives whose men ply the sea," reported the *New Bedford Standard-Times*. "Others went from boat to boat asking questions. Everywhere the answer was a simple negative shake of the head."

Across the river in Fairhaven, fifteen hundred were homeless. Seven bodies were found the next day; others remained buried amid piles of splintered homes. In nearby Harbor View, where unemployed factory workers tried to subsist by fishing, scores of flimsy shacks collapsed in the storm. In the initial reports, Greater New Bedford had sixty-nine dead, forty missing, and $5 million in damage.

Beaches along the southeastern Massachusetts coast were swept clean. Not a single home remained on East Rodney French Boulevard, a coastal road south of New Bedford. At Swift's Beach in Wareham, every cottage crumbled, and nine people died. Nine others died in Mattapoisett—most of them along Crescent Beach, where 160 of the 170 seaside cottages collapsed. With the exception of Marion (where Tabor Academy dormitories flooded onto the second floor, and where the entire Beverly Yacht Club washed into the sea), not a single coastal community escaped death.

As elsewhere, however, hurricane victims displayed fortitude amid the crisis. After the surge destroyed her Crescent Beach cottage, seventy-five-year-old Jennie Brown was buffeted by the tides while trapped in the cramped space under her demolished rooftop. Rescuers found her with the clothes ripped from her body and sixty-eight splinters lodged into her skin. But she outlasted the ordeal without any serious injury.

Arthur Small, the lighthouse keeper on Palmer's Island in New Bedford's harbor, was trying to reach his station when winds overturned his boat. His wife, whom he had left on high ground, tried to board a rowboat and save him.

Arthur saw the waves slam the boathouse, killing his wife. Grieving and injured by floating debris, he remained true to his profession's code, lighting the lamp and never abandoning his post. Commissioner Harold D. King of the Washington Bureau of Lighthouses later called it "one of the most outstanding cases of loyalty and devotion that has come to the attention of this office."

The hurricane had left an indelible stamp. September 21, 1938, was the first day of work for *New Bedford Standard-Times* reporter Everett S. Allen. His first memory of the hurricane was watching a woman get blown off her feet in front of City Hall. "What I remember of the next several hours is fragmented, some things sharply, some no more than impressions, and they tumble upon each other in confusion, which is the way they happened." The experience galvanized him; that day, he decided to remain a journalist. The experience also haunted him; almost forty years later, he wrote *A Wind to Shake the World*, the first complete history of the Hurricane of 1938.

❦   ❦   ❦

THE ISLANDS SOUTH OF CAPE COD absorbed the hurricane's full impact. "I lost everything except for what I stand in," said one dazed fisherman in Cuttyhunk, where the entire fishing village was leveled. The town wharf fell into the sea, and homes and boats drifted away. Eleven men had hoisted a new American flag above a new Coast Guard boathouse that morning. During the storm, the Coast Guard had to rescue the crew from atop a pile driver. The next day they found the flag not only shredded, but also tied into knots.

On Martha's Vineyard, coastal roads flooded at Vineyard Haven and Oak Bluffs. In Edgartown, the fishing fleet's moorings snapped, and the boats tumbled end over end out to sea. Menemsha Basin, the picturesque fishing harbor for Chilmark, got hit by three twenty-five-foot waves. Piers and fishing shacks had once huddled over the harbor, but after the storm there stood only some forlorn posts. A sand spit once crowded with boats and cottages had become an island—the storm had carved a channel through it, leaving just one shack, leaning precariously toward the harbor.

On Chilmark's South Beach, Josephine Clarke, a maid from Jamaica, lived with her employers, Benedict and Virginia Thielen. In the storm's prelude, streams trickled through the sturdy home, the sound of rolling pebbles built from innocent clicks into a threatening crescendo, and discolored frothy lumps—"like the vomit foam of a sick animal," according to Benedict—blew in from the sea. Clarke and the Thielens bundled in sweaters and boots, preparing to evacuate. They stepped off the back porch into a foot of water. Six steps later, the first surge landed, and they were soon neck-deep in water. Clarke could not swim; she drowned. The Thielens survived, but that night was torment. "The wind cries all night long around the house," Benedict recalled, "and every time you close your eyes you see the immense slavering arch of the oncoming wave, the yellow spittle dripping down, and a dead face in the sullied waters."

Most of Cape Cod escaped such tragedy. For sure, there was chaos: The region lost electricity and telephone service, and news from the mainland arrived only in person, from those who negotiated flooded, debris-strewn streets. Unfounded rumors swelled that thousands had died in Boston. Nevertheless, the dense summer crowds had already left the peninsula, Martha's Vineyard and Nantucket broke some of the surge's strength, and the lower Cape was far from the hurricane's eye.

But along Buzzards Bay, which divides the Cape from the mainland, the destruction was considerable. Like Narragansett Bay, Buzzards Bay captured and funneled the storm tides pushing up from the south, and the hurricane struck near high tide. One promontory in the bay measured tides almost fifteen feet above mean high water.

At Woods Hole, waves smashed the wharves and crashed over the seawall, flooding the village. The storm made an island out of Penzance Point, the site of multiple calamities. Two Coast Guardsmen died while trying to save a trapped family. An elderly caretaker named Albert Neal was boarding up doors and windows when the tides surged through Great Harbor, stranding him and his son, Milton. For two hours they hugged utility poles, but after a big wave, Albert lost his grip and drowned. Another caretaker, William Briggs, was in ankle-high water when a huge wave knocked him down. He got up, only for another wave to carry him into an inland marsh. Both a neighbor and Briggs's young son saw him die. "I could see his head for some distance," reported the neighbor. "He threw up his arms once or twice and then disappeared." His body was found two days later, covered in leaves and branches and splintered wood.

Silver Beach lies farther north along the bay. Here Mr. and Mrs. Andrew Jones died. They had been among the first to settle Silver Beach, in a waterfront cottage they called "The House That Jack Built." The previous year, they and four hundred friends had celebrated their golden wedding anniversary. As the hurricane intensified, the couple climbed onto the roof. When the house

National Guardsmen mourn the tragedy under the Bourne Bridge (courtesy of the Boston Public Library)

broke apart, neighbors unsuccessfully tried throwing them a lifeline of tied-together blankets. Then their floating roof crashed into another building, killing them both. The *Falmouth Enterprise* later ran a picture of their home's ruins, topped by an intact sign: "The House That Jack Built."

At the top of Buzzards Bay lies Bourne, the gateway to the Cape Cod Canal. The town's annual report that year would abandon its dry tone as it described the "raging gale": "the angry sea, irritated by the ceaseless winds, arose like one huge wave, and approached helpless nearby villages, as if to engulf the southern portion of the town in one gigantic mouthful." The worst tragedy occurred under the Bourne Bridge, in the swelled waters of the Canal, where a half-submerged house from two miles south had landed. Trapped inside were three elderly women and an eleven-year-old boy, none of whom could swim, along with Hayward Wilson, their neighbor and would-be rescuer. When a work force of policemen, firemen, and naval reservists broke through the roof, they found Wilson's body with a bruised, gashed forehead and hands. In a last-ditch effort, he had tried to smash an escape hatch through the ceiling. But he and the four others had drowned in the flooded second story.

ON THE MORNING OF SEPTEMBER 21, 1938, the people of Boston had many concerns: the surprise victory in the Democratic gubernatorial primary by the controversial James Michael Curley (he would lose the general election that November), the Red Sox's doubleheader sweep of the St. Louis Browns (Boston would finish nine and a half games behind the New York Yankees), and the annexation of the Sudetenland from Czechoslovakia by Adolf Hitler (he would start World War II). A small note in the *Boston Globe*'s evening edition mentioned a tropical storm over Connecticut.

At least one Bostonian saw the hurricane coming, however. E. B. Rideout was the beloved, quirky weatherman at radio station WEEI. He slept about four hours a night, pulled out weather charts while driving his car, and often paused on air until he found the appropriate scribbled note. But he never missed a broadcast, and on the rare occasion when he muffed a forecast, he denied himself pudding after his ritual lunch at Durgin Park. On September 21, Rideout saw the high-pressure systems flanking a zone of low pressure into New England and predicted the hurricane's eventual path. His fellow meteorologists scoffed. But after the storm, Rideout's listeners thanked him in spades. On September 22, he ate two puddings.

If only more people had listened to E. B. Rideout. The heavy winds arrived in Boston around 5:00, as people emerged from their offices. Pedestrians grabbed onto streetlamps and each other, shielding their faces from flying gravel. The plate-glass display windows along Tremont and Boylston Streets shattered. Falling trees brought down sputtering wires, blocked cobblestone streets and major highways, and impeded trains carrying home suburbanites—stranded passengers had to amuse themselves for hours by playing cards, singing, and speculating about the Czechoslovakian crisis. So many false alarms rang throughout the night that fire engines just cruised the streets looking for actual crises. Boston City Hospital treated three hundred storm-related injuries. At the Blue Hill Observatory, just miles from downtown Boston, the windmill anemometer disintegrated after recording a two-minute average wind speed of 83 miles per hour. Another anemometer recorded an average speed of 121 miles per hour over a five-minute span, and it measured a peak gust of 187 miles per hour.

Few in the tight-knit Italian community of the North End slept that night. Its small fleet of fishing boats was lost at sea. Not until dawn did reports of safe dockings—and tragic losses—start coming in. Frank Marino arrived

An uprooted tree on Arlington Street in downtown Boston, adjacent to the Public Garden (courtesy of the Boston Public Library)

home on Prince Street—his face cut, his teeth knocked loose, his body so exhausted that he could barely speak. After his boat capsized, a British steamer had thrown him a lifeline, but his three fellow crew members had died.

The tug *Mildred Olsen* overturned off Fish Pier in Boston Harbor. Dr. Floyd Rowland and his son, Ross, rowed a dory out to save the crew, but their boat overturned, too. Army personnel rescued the Rowlands and three of the tugboat's crew, but two others drowned. One of the bodies washed up the next morning on Malibu Beach in Dorchester.

In Dorchester Bay, entire fleets splintered as storm-tossed yachts smashed into stone walls and concrete landings. Sailboats on the Charles River drifted pell-mell, and one large pleasure craft blew ashore near Soldiers Field. At the Charlestown Navy Yard, the USS *Constitution* absorbed damage to its hull. At the airport in East Boston, an American Airlines transport plane had been moored outside with heavy cables due to lack of hangar space; the eight-ton aircraft blew 2,700 feet, just missed the corner of a building, crashed through a hundred feet of wire fence, and landed in a gully.

The historic green in Lexington, again rendered a battlefield (courtesy of the Boston Public Library)

"It was the funniest storm I ever saw," marveled Helen Whitley, who lived on Marlborough Street in the Back Bay. "Just wind that acted as if it had giant hands which grabbed and twisted everything they came in contact with, wrenching it up and throwing it down." Felled trees and storm debris scarred landmark public spaces: the Public Garden, Boston Common, Harvard Yard, the Charles River Embankment. The worst ecological damage was in the Arnold Arboretum, the city's repository of botanical treasures, where more than fifteen hundred trees were uprooted or snapped into pieces.

For a region steeped in history, Greater Boston took some historic blows. The town of Canton lost trees that had greeted the first Puritan arrivals. The Revolutionary battlefields at Concord and Lexington looked as if they had just staged battles. Farther west, officials in Groton labeled the Hurricane of 1938 "the most disastrous storm which probably ever visited this Town since the coming of the White man."

Margaret Eastman of North Woburn turned seven years old on September 21, 1938, and the hurricane ruled her birthday memories. Her family lived on the second and third floors of a drafty tenement house. Margaret stared out the windows, worrying whether her father, brother, and grandfather would arrive home safely. Before they all came back, Margaret's mother tried to soothe her by lighting her birthday cake. But the wind sliced through the walls, and the draft kept snuffing out the candle before she could make a wish.

Two men in North Attleboro died when the roof of the Sears Garage collapsed upon them. Falling trees killed men in Brockton and Watertown. A flying piazza roof killed an Everett man. Crumbling chimneys took the lives of men from both Malden and Hopedale; the latter man had been out searching for his stranded daughter.

"The sensible thing to have done was to have stayed in a solidly built building like ours, to wait for the storm to pass," recalled a factory owner in Worcester. "But not one of our employees did so." At first, most reacted with humor and amazement, not fear—they had no hurricane warnings and no hurricane experience. By that night, however, four people were dead, hundreds injured, and electricity and telephones out. A radio station repeated news bulletins and assurances to the surrounding communities. A dozen churches were rubble. The bells of the First Unitarian Church in Lincoln Square kept pealing as the clock hands whirled. The spire wobbled, righted itself, and then dropped, snapping the church's cross-beams and splitting the structure up the middle.

Some towns in central Massachusetts took severe economic wallops—particularly cruel setbacks in the midst of a depression. In Gardner, a town renowned for its furniture, hurricane winds ripped the roof and third story off a chair factory, displacing fifteen hundred workers. A plant in Athol also shut down after hurricane damage. In Southbridge, where the main streets resembled rivers and the Flats district had to be evacuated, the Ames Worsted Company flooded after a dam burst. Fitchburg averted a similar tragedy thanks to a massive flood control project that the federal government had instituted after the 1936 flood. In 1938, the dam held up, saving the city's lower section.

The Hurricane of 1938 delivered devastation to families, homes, businesses, and communities. William Zielinski, a Lowell poultry dealer, told a policeman that the wind had overturned his chicken cages, hurting his business. The officer asked why he was not searching for them. "I will," Zielinski snapped back, "but give me time. Right now I'm looking for the roof of my house."

❧ ❧ ❧

THE STORM STRUCK WESTERN MASSACHUSETTS much as it had inland Connecticut. The Connecticut River and its tributaries were already flooding after four days of heavy rain. The hurricane continued north along the same moist highway, bringing a devastating combination of winds and flood.

Springfield was in crisis by the night of the storm. Eight-foot whitecaps raged up the Connecticut River. Buses, trains, and cars had stalled. Fallen trees and downed power lines covered the fractured pavement of city streets. A ferris wheel at an annual fair toppled. And the river kept rising. The mayor ordered the South End evacuated at 9:30 P.M. Twenty guards, a dozen deputy sheriffs, and a militia company escorted two hundred fifty prisoners from Hampden County Jail to temporary quarters at the Springfield College gymnasium. Three thousand city residents spent the night in schools, churches, and government buildings as a crew saved the dike in the North End, dragging sandbags across dark and ravaged streets.

Floodwaters poured through Chicopee's industrial center, ruining factories, putting thousands out of work, and forcing the evacuation of some waterfront neighborhoods. Four hundred families evacuated South Holyoke, where the swelling Connecticut River destroyed the city's paper mills. The tiny village of Three Rivers was under water, and thirty-four families saw all their worldly possessions swept away.

Farmers fared no better than factory workers. One farmer recalled that when the hurricane struck his hilltop orchard, "apples filled the air like buckshot." One million apples—about half the total crop—were blown from their trees, and the entire peach crop was on the ground. The earlier flooding had already ruined the onion crop, and more than half the region's tobacco barns collapsed. Many tobacco farmers had prepared for the storm by propping up the north side of their barns, since the hurricane was coming from the south. But where the eye passed to the east, the strong winds came from the north, and the props were useless.

The hurricane isolated the towns of the Berkshires. The Cold River ate chunks out of the Mohawk Trail, the major road through northwestern Massachusetts. Streams running down the Greylock and Hoosac mountain ranges swept through the main streets of Adams. A landslide near Zoar tore up a thousand feet of railroad track. Of the thirty-six bridges in Charlemont, only four survived.

In western Massachusetts, too, the hurricane stole young lives. At Northfield Seminary, near the New Hampshire and Vermont borders, 140 teenage girls were eating dinner at Gould Hall. At 6:15, the hall's brick chimney started crumbling from the top. It fell through the roof, crashing through a skylight and raining bricks across the dining room. Many girls suffered cuts and bruises, and faculty and staff had to escort fifteen girls to the hospital in Greenfield—a slow journey across tree-strewn roads. For Norma Stockberger and Audrey Lucas, it was too late. Both girls had died instantly.

∞ ∞ ∞

NEW HAMPSHIRE'S SOUTHWEST CORNER HAD SUFFERED extensive flooding before the hurricane struck. A landslide smothered a railroad line between Ashuelot and Hinsdale. Keene was isolated. The streams and rivers surrounding Jaffrey were double their normal height, and the morning of the storm, floods had washed out a temporary coffer dam and the village's one-day-old bridge.

The hurricane drove the rising water into swells. In Hillsborough, the double-arched bridge over the Contoocook River collapsed, and flooding destroyed the town's hosiery mill. In Jaffrey, a boathouse caved into high bubbling waters; it floated across a road and settled there, blocking traffic to nearby Squantum. In Keene, the storm obliterated the economic mainstays: lumberyards, textile mills, a golf tee factory.

No town in New Hampshire confronted more chaos than fire-plagued Peterborough. The Contoocook had spilled into bins of unslaked lime at the Farmers Grain Company, sparking a fire around 4:30 P.M. The fastest winds arrived soon after, whipping sparks and igniting more fires across the mill town. By the time the fire department had fought across an overflowing river and flooded roads, it was a full-blown disaster. No one in Peterborough died or was seriously injured, but the fire had incinerated four business blocks, including the grain mill, two garages, a market, and the plant of the *Peterborough Transcript*.

In North Weare, four women, ranging in age from fifty-five to eighty, had been watching the torrential Piscataquog River from a bridge along the state road. After a dam collapsed in Deering, the waters rushed down the valley to the reservoir in Weare, where they knocked through the concrete core of another dam. The instant onrush wiped out the bridge before the women could escape. Three of them died when the bridge collapsed. A fourth survived the fall. She grabbed onto a beam, and she surged through the white-water melee. Then a log struck her in the head, and she died, too.

Amidst such tragedy, at least there were stories of hope. In Wentworth, a woman went into labor on the night of September 21. Her nurse walked alone for a half-mile, through fierce winds and over and under storm debris, before reaching a road, where a truck took her to the mother's home. By then electricity and telephones were out. Eight men needed three hours to reach the family physician in Warren. By the time the doctor arrived at the home, it was too late. By the light of oil lamps and candles, at 10:01 P.M., Joan Morrison was born—a healthy hurricane baby.

THE HURRICANE HAD MAINTAINED exceptional strength as it traveled inland. It started to weaken only after the eye passed through southwest New Hampshire—at that point, the hurricane could no longer pull up warm water, and colder night air swirled into the vortex. But before the storm petered out, it left its mark on Vermont.

At least seven people in Vermont died, most by drowning. The state's southern half experienced overflowing rivers and flood damage. In Grafton, eleven bridges collapsed into the Saxtons River. Further north, Montpelier had no flooding, but the winds were strong enough to ravage the Pavilion Building. The historic structure's chimney crashed through its roof, raining bricks upon guests in the building's hotel. As the winds howled and power lines hissed, the surreality of a Caribbean storm in the Green Mountains seemed difficult to register. In the building's basement grill, reported one man, "people were dining and drinking by candlelight, chatting casually and lighting cigarettes from the flames. It was somewhat what you would imagine war days to be like—tenseness beneath light laughter and gayety."

As far north as Newport, near the Canadian border, the storm cut out telephones, telegraphs, and electricity. The winds and rain arrived there around 8:00, and they lasted until midnight. Barns crumpled, shingles rocketed off homes, and metal roofs twisted into bizarre sculptures. People later found their roofs in adjacent towns. The storm continued into Quebec, leveling fields and tossing the fruit off orchard trees. Then it turned northwest toward Montreal. Finally, in the early morning hours of September 22, the swirling phenomenon of screeching wind, warm stinging rain, and wanton destruction dwindled in upon itself. The Hurricane of 1938 was over.

CHAPTER SIX

Aftermath

THERE IS NO MORE beautiful weather than in hurricane season when you're not having a hurricane," Ernest Hemingway would later write in *The Old Man and the Sea*. New England might not have such a season, but September 22, 1938, dawned fresh and brilliant, as if the hurricane had vacuumed up a gloomy shroud. Now the sun shone upon a landscape strewn with wreckage, a people reckoning with their dead, a region confronting new challenges.

Slowly, the scale of calamity grew apparent. By Thursday evening, 243 were known dead. Each day the numbers of missing shrank, and the death tolls correspondingly rose. Although final totals are difficult to gauge, one accepted estimate is that the hurricane killed 680 people and caused $400 million in damage. (By comparison, the 1906 San Francisco Earthquake killed 450 people and cost $350 million, and the 1871 Chicago Fire caused 200 deaths and $200 million in property damage.) The experience slowly sank into the survivors' psyches. When newsreel footage appeared the following week, it trumped anything Sam Goldwyn and John Ford had ever managed in *The Hurricane*.

"The smell of bodies!" recalled Everett Allen. "In places, you could taste it in the food and it came through closed windows into your bedroom at night." The cleanup effort could challenge one's inner fortitude. From the Rhode Island coast, author Frances Woodward described a typical sensation: "Strange

Drying out pants on Cape Cod (courtesy of the Boston Public Library)

to poke in filthy rubbish, trying to find your clothes, or your spoons, or maybe part of your tool chest, and turn up a painted tray nobody had ever seen before. Funny how bad the smell was, when you always thought of the sea and the sand as so clean." A salty spray traveled inland, burning the vegetation left standing. Some recalled the smell of raw wood from all the cracked-open trees. Within days, it smelled mostly of rotting leaves.

The wreckage compelled neighbors to band together to seek solutions. Throughout the region people collected clothes and food, nursed the wounded, and sheltered the newly homeless. They cleaned up the streets together. Some hoped that the hurricane had blown away selfishness and greed. "It brought people together," remembered David Molloy of Providence. "They helped each other out and really cared." A pastor from his city agreed, arguing that the storm had produced "a democracy of suffering," because rich and poor alike had endured the crisis. The hurricane showed the common bonds of humanity and revealed the natural superiority of democracy—a contention with extra resonance in the shadow of the Czechoslovakian crisis. But the storm's rubble also raised new questions. Who paid when one neighbor's tree crashed through the other neighbor's fence? Who got to keep the wood?

Confusion and rumors seeped through every crack. New Englanders were so unfamiliar with hurricanes that G. Harold Noyes, chief of the Boston Weather Bureau, felt compelled to announce that the storm would not return. With communication lines down and towns isolated, radio stations and newspapers could only relay scattered reports of the calamities elsewhere. Separating truth from gossip was difficult. On the Rhode Island coast many believed that everyone on Block Island had died. People also passed on grisly tidbits: In pockets of South County, there were not enough blankets to cover all the dead bodies. A telegraph from the Red Cross office in Norwich, Connecticut, indicated the scale of trauma: "Food supply exhausted. Five hundred families now being fed and housed. Complete isolation. No outside help available as yet. Need food and clothing. Serum has been sent from Hartford."

Europe may have been on the brink of war, but Long Island and New England had fought a one-day battle against an invincible foe. From that defeat emerged lessons. The survivors emerged with a new respect for nature, a new appreciation of its capricious hand. They sought solutions through government and technology, speeding the country's evolution to a modern world. And they showed how a crisis can be a crucible of character, exposing humanity at its best and its worst.

❧   ❧   ❧

EVEN AS THE WINDS STILL HOWLED—as car horns honked, as solitary candles flickered in scattered windows, and as the flooded streets of downtown Providence still churned with the ominous shadows of the storm's debris—the looting began. Looters held flashlights above the murky waters, and they climbed through shattered windows, stealing everything from jewelry to five-cent pencils, packing their contraband in rowboats and burlap sacks. The trickle of rogues turned into a horde. "They seemed organized, almost regimented, as if they'd daily drilled and prepared for this event," wrote David Cornel DeJong. "They were brazen and insatiable; they swarmed like rats." Even after policemen arrived in a rowboat, the looters kept on, aware that they outnumbered the police. As the waters drained away, the looters only grew bolder, smashing the windows that the wind had spared. Lawlessness reigned; there were also reports of sexual assaults on women.

The next morning, at the Savin Hill Yacht Club south of Boston, four hundred people stripped the boats blown ashore—at least until fifty policemen arrived to scatter the mob. In Woods Hole, a woman described an all-too-typical scene: Two gruff men were rummaging around a washed-up boathouse. She reported their license number to the police, who stopped the pair's vehicle and found the trunk stuffed with booty.

The states responded by imposing martial law. Rhode Island called out its State Guard an hour after the hurricane struck. By 9:00 that night, 150 guardsmen were restoring order in downtown Providence, and they arrested seven suspected looters. They also shot huge antiaircraft searchlights down the main streets, casting shadows off an eerie blue glare. By the next week, they had arrested fifty-nine looters throughout Rhode Island. In the afflicted coastal communities, the National Guard issued access passes to areas with hurricane damage, halting throngs of sightseers as well as potential criminals. In the worst-hit regions, martial law remained in effect for weeks afterward.

The looters—"Jackals of the Storm," in the words of the *Providence Bulletin*—were cravenly persistent, especially in Massachusetts. Days after the hurricane, bands of looters sped along the eastern coast of Buzzards Bay, hauling off valuables in vans and boats. Adjutant General Charles H. Cole responded in the extreme: He issued "shoot to kill" orders for all looters on the Cape. The situation degenerated. Days later, soldiers fired at looters in Bourne. At Menauhant Beach in Falmouth, a rifle bullet just missed two patrolling guardsmen. In North Falmouth, a speeding car with no license plate nearly ran down the soldier on duty at a checkpoint.

The looters embodied greed, lawlessness, and audaciousness. Perhaps they also revealed a desperation unique to the Great Depression, for the hurricane had struck some brutal economic blows. Almost no one had hurricane insurance policies. The repair of public spaces meant hikes in local tax rates. And storm damage put people out of work, especially the farmers and factory workers still tasting the Great Depression. Many plants, already on flimsy economic footings, had to suspend operations and leave workers without wages. Some, such as the American Thread Company in Pawcatuck, Connecticut, shut down for good. The crisis was perhaps worse in agriculture. As fruit and fallen trees littered the ground, some farmers abandoned their orchards forever. One central Massachusetts man surveyed the damage, walked down to his cellar, and hanged himself.

Though many officials from the Washington, D.C., headquarters had gone to Florida for the expected hurricane, the Red Cross quickly set up emergency shelters in Hartford, Springfield, and Chicopee. They took in more than

15,000 refugees, provided first aid to 6,000 people, and gave 11,000 inoculations against disease. Nearly 20,000 families appealed to the Red Cross for help, and the organization distributed $1.6 million in aid. Their massive rehabilitation effort included repairing and rebuilding homes, providing medical care for the injured, repairing and replacing the equipment for small fishermen, and restoring the fields of small farmers.

But the Hurricane of 1938 cost more than any single organization could handle. The recovery effort demanded money and manpower on a huge scale, and the federal government answered that demand—a function made possible by the crisis of the Great Depression. The New Deal, in its efforts to provide security and jump-start the economy, employed millions of workers (whether necessary or not) in a variety of public works projects through such agencies as the Works Progress Administration (WPA). As of September 1938, the WPA had a hundred thousand people from New England and Long Island on its active payrolls.

By the afternoon of Friday, September 23, the WPA was hiring virtually all its available men off relief rolls, and the workers began clearing the streets so that supply trucks and repair crews could do their work. Ten thousand workers from the Civilian Conservation Corps, which employed young men in forestry and flood control programs, cleared streets and helped save flood-threatened areas in Connecticut and Massachusetts. The National Youth Administration, a federal organization that found part-time work for men between the ages of sixteen and twenty-five, supplied thousands of workers for cleaning and salvaging projects. The Reconstruction Finance Corporation lent funds to damaged businesses. The Federal Power Commission sent engineers to help restore electrical service. The Federal Surplus Commodities Corporation provided food and supplies to needy areas. Even the Federal Writers' Project, a branch of the WPA, commissioned a pictorial history of the disaster.

On Sunday, September 25, the governors of New England met at Boston's Copley Hotel with Harry Hopkins, national director of the WPA. They asked Hopkins for $75 million from the WPA coffers. "There are sufficient funds to meet this emergency," Hopkins assured. "We will do whatever needs to be done." In the weeks to come, federal workers cleaned the beaches of bodies and debris, and they strengthened the dikes that held floodwaters. Mills and factories began to reopen, and the trains started running again.

Not everyone appreciated the help. Arthur Raynor of Westhampton, Long Island, later moaned about "the Roosevelt boondoggle." He presumed that his

Hurricane damage in the village of East Hampton, Long Island (courtesy of the East Hampton Library)

village quickly received a "jillion" WPA workers because President Roosevelt often came to visit his old law partner, Basil O'Connor. Raynor ran a crew "and couldn't get a day's work out of the lot of them." He echoed a familiar criticism of the New Deal's propensity to foster idleness and complacency among the work force.

Whatever one's opinion on the New Deal, the hurricane revealed a larger redefinition of American politics. Not just on the federal level, but also in such states as Massachusetts, Connecticut, and Rhode Island, the legislatures and executive offices had long been dominated by the Republican Party, built on a foundation of fiscal conservatism and an old-stock, Yankee sensibility. But the large-scale immigration of the late nineteenth and early twentieth centuries, combined with the crisis of the Depression, spurred a Democratic ascendancy. With that political shift, the government's responsibility expanded. By 1938 the federal government existed not only to protect basic rights, but also to shape the world of its citizens—especially in times of hardship.

Previous disasters in American history had spurred large private relief efforts. The Relief and Aid Society, a private organization, had overseen relief for the victims of the Great Chicago Fire. Newspaper publisher William Randolph Hearst, among others, had organized immense fund-raising drives for victims of the Galveston Hurricane and the San Francisco Earthquake. Though the Red Cross organized a charitable campaign for the 1938 hurricane victims, New Deal organizations supplied the overwhelming bulk of funds for relief and recovery. That the government rather than private citizens rebuilt New England and Long Island spoke not only to the economic hardships of the Depression, but also to the transformation of American political culture.

✺ ✺ ✺

IN THE SHORT TERM, the hurricane cast New England into a simpler time. People used candles for light and fireplaces for cooking. To avoid contamination, drinking water had to be boiled. Some celebrated that their towns, isolated by blocked roads and burdened by shared plights, had restored the communal spirit of an era long past. There were clever innovations, such as the gas station owner who removed a rear bicycle wheel and ran a belt over the pump's pulley, so that a teenager could pedal up gas from the tank. But the hurricane also produced crises that demanded modern solutions.

One crisis was in the timber industry. The hurricane had blown down an estimated three billion board feet of timber, and this wood threatened to flood the market. Some landowners tipped their logs into ponds, trying to preserve them until prices rose. The federal government intervened: The United States Forest Service established the New England Forest Emergency Project, and the Reconstruction Finance Corporation set up the Northeastern Timber Salvage Corporation. These organizations installed sawmills to salvage felled timber, paid workers to clear debris, and established nurseries to nourish new forests. They also bought timber at prices above the depressed market value. The government helped stave off disaster, and the timber industry rebounded with the skyrocketing demand after World War II began.

Felled trees and power lines still stymied communication and productivity. For days after September 21, tree-choked roads trapped many citizens within their towns. Traffic piled up around Boston when many people ignored police warnings of closed roads. Along the Connecticut coast, according to New Haven Railroad authorities, "miles of silent track hung at crazy angles over yawning chasms in a hopeless tangle of power lines, signal towers, houses, boats, and thousands of tons of debris." New York City's Grand Central Station filled with would-be travelers to Springfield, Worcester, and Boston, including returning college students set to begin the fall term.

A special delivery of mud for a mailman in Ware, Massachusetts (courtesy of the Boston Public Library)

With trains unable to deliver New England its mounting piles of mail, the battleship *Wyoming* carried 14,000 sacks of mail from New York City to Boston Harbor, and another 7,000 sacks arrived from Savannah, Georgia; 200 WPA workers sorted this mail and the South Boston post office hired 150 extra postmen. Amateur ham radio operators worked for nearly two weeks from the State House in Providence, passing on death notices, health updates, information on embalmers and caskets, and the course of relief operations. Also, to bypass unusable roads and railroads, businessmen flocked to the airlines, then still in their fledgling state. So many passengers demanded flights along the New York–Boston route that American Airlines invited competitors to break its monopoly. Until train service was completely restored on October 1, the airlines carried 8,000 passengers, many of whom flew for the first time.

The hurricane also posed the greatest challenge in the history of the local power and telephone companies. In southern New England, 536,555 customers—88 percent of the total—lost power. About one-fourth of all New England's telephones were knocked out. There was little direct communication with the rest of the United States, except through radio. The storm brought down 72 million feet of wire, damaged 400 miles of underground cable, and felled 31,000 poles. And because of the crisis, operators had to field five times the normal number of calls from New England.

Despite the lack of warning, the power and telephone companies conducted a massive restoration effort. Telephone calls to New York were routed through cable lines to and from Europe. The New England Power Association first restored power at hospitals, pumping stations, fire alarm systems, and water purification plants. On top of its 2,600 regular crewmen, the company hired another 2,000 part-time and emergency workers. Power and telephone repairmen, originally on reserve in case the hurricane hit Florida, instead arrived in New England from twenty other states, including Virginia, Texas, and South Dakota. The crisis even spawned a challenge to gender roles: Men from Bell Telephone's accounting department worked as emergency operators, startling callers accustomed to hearing female voices.

IN THE WEEKS AFTER SEPTEMBER 21, a beggar marched through Boston Common wearing a sandwich board: "For twenty-five cents I'll listen to your story of the hurricane." Everyone had a story, and each revealed some aspect of the hurricane's impact: its power, its tragedy, its ability to reshape human relations. To tour the stricken regions was to learn something of this history.

Early Thursday morning in Quogue, Long Island, the village trustees called an emergency meeting and appointed fire chief Sid Phillips the town marshal. "He was the highest authority during the emergency," recalled one village resident, "and everyone had to answer to him." Amid the crisis, expediency outweighed custom. For three weeks, armed guards patrolled the main streets, and Phillips declared a 6:00 P.M. curfew. Cleanup workers and business owners needed passes to enter and exit the village. School was canceled. Phillips had Richard Beckwith and Herbie Philips drive trucks that hauled felled trees, even though neither fifteen-year-old boy had his license.

Harrison McDonald had spent the night on a swaying Pullman car outside Hartford. He arrived in New London by bus on Thursday morning. A National Guardsman handed him a card warning not to drink water or milk without boiling it. Outside a ruined five-and-ten store, the owner sold candles. Firemen in the business district were still hosing down embers. McDonald walked into a Western Union office, where a distraught woman sought news on her missing younger sister. A businessman wanted to send a wire to New York, but all lines were down. "Well, I don't suppose it's essential," he said. "I'd just like to let my company in New York know that they haven't got any New London factory any more. It's not a problem of damage, but one of complete abolition."

Upstate, the Connecticut River did not begin retreating until late Friday night, more than forty-eight hours after the hurricane. More than seven thousand people had evacuated Hartford during the crisis, and many stayed at the WPA's refugee centers, where the Federal Music Project entertained the evacuees. Naval militiamen used rowboats to ferry butchers across flooded streets, so that the butchers could dress four tons of meat for the refugees. Finally, on Saturday, the downtown lakes started draining away.

The Rhode Island coast paid the stiffest price, and it struggled to restore order. Streams of people entered Westerly Hospital. Those arriving later came with more serious injuries, as they had been trapped in the debris for hours, even days. On Watch Hill, a volunteer force with clubs and revolvers protected the remains of wealthy cottages until the National Guard arrived; all along the coast, police stations became emergency headquarters. Westerly High School became a central clearinghouse for corpses. There, families identified the bodies and chose funeral directors. Harold Kenyon, a twenty-four-year-old embalmer in Westerly, worked around the clock for the next five days, handling almost forty funerals. "It was so confusing," he remembered. "You didn't have time for feelings."

The streets of Providence flooded again the morning after the hurricane, but this time because firemen were pumping water out of store basements. Business owners, waiters, clerks, bootblacks, and hundreds of others donned grungy clothes and pulled sodden, silt-covered trash up to the sidewalks. As elsewhere, the State Guard posted warnings to boil water and avoid fallen wires, and it established refugee stations. After the initial cleanup, the city instituted a curfew and issued passes for downtown workers. Downtown remained dark for eleven days, causing confusing traffic snarls at busy intersections. The four major banks had to dry soggy documents and stock certificates through large electrical mangles, slowly allaying clients who had their life savings in safe deposit boxes. In the evenings, when the department stores and movie houses usually filled up, the city instead had a tragic, defeated air.

The Massachusetts legislature appropriated disaster funds, allocating $8.75 million to rebuild town and county roads, $5.5 million for state highways, and $3,432,414.92 for such state services as the militia and forest conservation. The rebuilding effort manipulated time itself; to create more working hours, Governor Charles Hurley requested an extension of daylight saving time.

A canoe washed up at Exchange Place in downtown Providence (courtesy of the Providence Public Library)

In western Massachusetts, no town endured as difficult an aftermath as Ware. In this town of eight thousand, the waters rose six feet higher than during the 1936 flood, leaving six hundred families homeless and causing $916,000 in damage. The water so tore up Main Street that it exposed the underlying sewer pipes. Worst of all, the three bridges connecting Ware to the outside world collapsed. For the next five days, planes dropped bread and serum into the stranded town. Two young Longmeadow couples first heard the distress signals on their radio; throughout the rescue operation, alternating duty around the clock, they relayed messages to the adjutant general's office in the State House. As elsewhere, ordinary citizens were performing extraordinary public duties.

New Hampshire and Vermont shared the same problems of contaminated water, downed power lines, and jungles of leaves and branches strewn across roads. Here, too, the rehabilitation effort compelled a spirit of fortitude. "Peterborough Can't Be Licked!" proclaimed the *Peterborough Transcript*—the day after its own building had disintegrated in the fire. The newspaper office had moved to a room in a nearby bank building.

In the White Mountains, where the writer Fairfax Downey and his family were still vacationing, there was destruction: "Every few yards, barring and crisscrossing, lay great trees—pines, birches, maples, elms—shattered, riven, rent asunder or wrenched bodily from the soil that their earth-covered roots towered twice as tall as a man. Only in a certain shell-torn woods in France had the Author seen worse devastation."Yet a mood of friendship and cooperation infused the cleanup effort, as neighbors came together to clear the road. While they worked, the radio warned of imminent war in Czechoslovakia. "Again the sober looks went around, and mouths tightened grimly. Bad business, war. They shouldered their axes and moved off. Still plenty of work to be done."

"It was a nobler war," mused Downey, "the war these sturdy New Englanders were waging against the ravages of the elements, standing neighbor by neighbor."

WAR SHAPED THE MEMORY OF THE HURRICANE OF 1938. Newspapers outside New England paid the storm little mind, and within days even the local media had shifted their attention. The hurricane drifted to the margins of the American consciousness. People instead focused on the world-encompassing zero hour, the clash between fascism and democracy.

Even on September 22, the hurricane shared front-page headlines in the *New York Times* with the European crisis. The Czechoslovakian government had just agreed to an Anglo-French partition plan that awarded the Sudetenland to Nazi Germany. Grown men—veterans of the Czech Legion from World War I—wept in public. British Prime Minister Neville Chamberlain flew to Germany for more negotiations with Adolf Hitler. But Hitler did not want concessions. In the days ahead, he demanded immediate annexation of the Sudetenland and recognition of Polish and Hungarian claims on Czechoslovakia, further weakening the central European bastion of democracy. Italian dictator Benito Mussolini demanded Hungarian territory to preserve his own prestige; the Czechoslovakian army mobilized; the French government called up five hundred thousand reservists; the British started digging air-raid shelters and learning how to use gas masks.

The United States remained an outside observer—a nation steeped in isolationism, and a nonfactor in European diplomacy. But the crisis riveted public attention. The Great Depression had already challenged the foundations of American democracy, and now, in Europe, fascism seemed increasingly indomitable. The next week, at a third conference in Munich, Britain and France capitulated to Hitler's demands for annexation. Chamberlain famously declared that they had achieved "peace in our time," but by March 1939 Germany had conquered Czechoslovakia, and that September Germany invaded Poland, igniting World War II. The Czechoslovakian crisis also started the slow erosion of American isolationism, a process that ended with the Japanese attack on Pearl Harbor in December 1941.

The Hurricane of 1938 was bound together with the stories of both the Great Depression and World War II, yet it fits neatly into neither narrative. New England was no Dust Bowl, where Depression-era poverty was most grim, so the storm never developed into an iconic instance of American history in the 1930s. Moreover, the onset of World War II detracted rather than focused attention upon the hurricane, so it never approached the mythological status of the Great Chicago Fire or the San Francisco Earthquake—natural disasters that have become rooted in the identities of their respective cities.

Hurricanes would strike New England again. In 1954, Hurricane Carol killed sixty-five people in Rhode Island, coastal Connecticut, and eastern Massachusetts. Hurricanes Diane in 1955, Donna in 1960, Gloria in 1985, and Bob in 1991 also touched New England. None, however, matched the might of the Hurricane of 1938. No natural disaster has killed more people in the region. It cost lives, homes, even faith. One hundred and seventy-five churches suffered damage, and six were utterly destroyed. Many churches moved services to temporary quarters. "At present we feel stunned," reported one Unitarian minister after the storm. He had enough funds to fix the structure, but not the spire. "It seems like the last blow to our church to which we have hung so desperately." He canceled services that Sunday, and he seemed uncertain about the future.

Others saw a greater meaning. Another minister proclaimed that "God is not dead. . . . We shall rise above the ruins." Indeed, the wreckage was cleared, the homes repaired, the trees replanted, the houses of worship of every faith rebuilt. And over the course of 1939, 1940, and 1941, their spires again soared above village greens, where some had reigned since the seventeenth century.

"I do not consider it a judgment of God," said the Reverend William Moe of the First Congregational Church in Guilford, Connecticut, as his church held a rededication ceremony. He answered a question that many had posed when the hurricane struck. Now he saw new possibilities, that "these conditions may form a stepping stone to something more permanent and enduring." Moe meant his message for his specific congregation, but he spoke a larger truth about the Hurricane of 1938. It had posed tests of the government, of technology, and of personal character. Some had failed, and others had triumphed.

SOURCES

THERE ARE TWO FINE BOOKS on the Hurricane of 1938. Everett S. Allen's *A Wind to Shake the World: The Story of the 1938 Hurricane* (Boston: Little, Brown, 1976) provides a comprehensive account of the destruction, and it often allows the storm's survivors to speak for themselves. R. A. Scotti's *Sudden Sea: The Great Hurricane of 1938* (Boston: Little, Brown, 2003) tells particular stories—the mismanagement of the Weather Bureau, the ordeal of the Moores at Watch Hill, the bus tragedy on Conanicut Island—with a novelist's eye for detail and drama. I have relied heavily on both sources. This short book hopefully adds a sense of historic context without shortchanging either the power of the hurricane or the personal narratives of its victims.

Any researcher of this storm should begin at the Massachusetts Historical Society, home of the Hildreth Parker Hurricane Collection. Volumes 43–85 and 118–130 focus on the Hurricane of 1938, and they include a wealth of sources: magazine articles, newspaper clippings, towns' annual reports, state government hearings, Red Cross publications, and more. The Boston Public Library, the Rhode Island Historical Society, the Providence Public Library, the Connecticut Historical Society, and the East Hampton Library also have important collections of archival materials and photographs.

The following paragraphs indicate key sources for some main stories in each chapter.

Chapter One: Onset

THE BURGHARDS' STORY is from a special commemorative issue of the *Hampton Chronicle* on September 26, 1968. See also Ernest Clowes, *The Hurricane of 1938 on Eastern Long Island* (Bridgehampton, N.Y.: Hampton Press, 1939), 27–28, and Allen, *A Wind to Shake the World*, 56–72.

On the storm's cost and destruction, see William Elliott Minsinger, ed., *The 1938 Hurricane: An Historical and Pictorial Summary* (Milton, Mass.: Blue Hill Observatory, 1988), 10–11, and American National Red Cross, *New York–New England Hurricane and Floods–1938: Official Report of Relief Operations* (Washington, D.C., 1938), 1–2. Other important histories are Federal Writers' Project of the Works Progress Administration, *New England Hurricane: A Factual, Pictorial Record* (Boston: Hale, Cushman, and Flint,

1938) and *The Complete Historical Record of New England's Stricken Area: September 21, 1938* (New Bedford, Mass.: Dean Publishing, 1939). The quotations from the Long Island farmhand and Ernest Clowes come from Clowes, *The Hurricane of 1938 on Eastern Long Island*.

For overviews of the Depression, the New Deal, and American foreign affairs leading to World War II, see David M. Kennedy, *Freedom from Fear: The American People in Depression and War, 1929–1945* (New York: Oxford University Press, 1999) and William Manchester, *The Glory and the Dream: A Narrative History of America, 1932–1972* (New York: Bantam Books, 1974). (Manchester also gives an entertaining history of the hurricane on pages 183–188.) For the Herbert Hoover quotations that liken the Depression to a hurricane, see Herbert Hoover, *The Memoirs of Herbert Hoover, Volume 3: The Great Depression, 1929–1941* (New York: Macmillan, 1952), 35–36, and http://americanhistory.about.com/library/docs.blhooverspeech1932. On the film *The Hurricane*, see A. Scott Berg, *Goldwyn: A Biography* (New York: Knopf, 1989), 294–297, and Joseph McBride, *Searching for John Ford: A Life* (New York: St. Martin's Press, 2001), 264–266.

Chapter Two: Into New York

THE OPENING EDITORIAL is from the *New York Times* on September 21, 1938.

On hurricane formation, see Jack Williams, *The Weather Book: An Easy-to-Understand Guide to the USA's Weather*, 2nd ed. (New York: Vintage, 1997); Robert H. Simpson and Herbert Riehl, *The Hurricane and Its Impact* (Baton Rouge: Louisana State University Press, 1981); Roger A. Pielke Jr. and Roger A. Pielke Sr., *Hurricanes: Their Nature and Impacts on Society* (West Sussex, England: John Wiley, 1997).

On the course of the Hurricane of 1938 and the formation of storm surges, see Gardner Emmons, "The Meteorological Aspects of the New England Hurricane," *The Collecting Net*, March 1939, 1–9; I. R. Tannehill, "The Recent Hurricane in New England," *Scientific Monthly*, December 1938, 42–50; and David M. Ludlum, "The Great Hurricane of 1938," *Weatherwise*, August 1988, 214–16. Also see these following Web sites:

www.intellicast.com/DrDewpoint/Library/1123

www2.sunysuffolk.edu/mandias/38hurricane

www.erh.noaa.gov/nerfc/historical/sept1938

The story of the Stockbridge, Massachusetts, man is from John Q. Stewart, "New England Hurricane," *Harper's*, January 1939, 203.

On Charles Pierce and the Weather Bureau, see Scotti, *Sudden Sea*, 71–77; Minsinger, *The 1938 Hurricane*, 24–27; *Bulletin for the American Meteorological Society* 76 (10), October 1995, 1838. On previous hurricanes in New England, see Minsinger, *The 1938 Hurricane*, 16–21, and F. Barrows Colton, "The Geography of a Hurricane," *National Geographic*, April 1939, 530–531. See also U.S. Department of Commerce, *Some Devastating North Atlantic Hurricanes of the 20th Century* (Washington, D.C., 1970).

On the destruction along the Jersey Shore, Westchester County, and New York City, see the *New York Times*, September 22–23, 1938.

The story from Pond Point, some of the tidbits of survival on Westhampton Beach, stories of destruction throughout the Hamptons, and the impact on the fishing industry come from Clowes, *The Hurricane of 1938 on Eastern Long Island*. General accounts of the storm's impact also appear in Federal Writers' Project, *New England Hurricane*, 9–13. The stories of the Greenes, the Shuttlesworths, and the Peterses come from Quogue Historical Society, *The 1938 Hurricane as We Remember It*, Vol. II (Quogue, N.Y., 1998). On the Shuttlesworths see also the transcript of the PBS documentary *The 1938 Hurricane as We Remember It*, Vol. II, available at www.pbs.org/wgbh/amex/hurricane38.

The story of the countess and her butler is from the *Boston Globe*, September 23, 1938. The legend of the man and his barometer is from Joe McCarthy, "Hurricane of '38," *American Heritage*, August 1969, 11. The environmental impact on Long Island is detailed in Arthur David Howard, "Hurricane Modification of the Offshore Bar of Long Island, New York," *The Geographical Review* 29(3), July 1939: 400–415. See also Norm Dvoskin, "A Weathercaster's Survey of Long Island's Climate and Historic Storms," *Long Island Historical Journal* 5 (1), 1992, 67–80; *Time*, October 3, 1938; and the *New York Times*, September 22–23, 1938.

The Long Island Collection at the East Hampton Library has other sources on the hurricane in Long Island: Margaret B. Perry, *The 1938 Hurricane as We Remember It* (Quogue, N.Y.: Quogue Historical Society, 1988); June Hess Kelly, *Scrapbook of the 1938 Hurricane, with Clippings and Photographs* (1938); Roger K. Brickner, *The Long Island Express* (Batavia, N.Y.: Hodgins, 1988).

Chapter Three: Connecticut

THE STORY OF THE FLOATING fuel tank in New Haven is from Leslie H. Tyler, *The New England Hurricane: An Album of Pictures of the Hurricane and Floods* (New Haven: City Printing, 1938). For accounts of the devastation throughout Connecticut, see the *Hartford* Courant, September 22–23, 1938.

On Katharine Hepburn and Old Saybrook, see Scotti, *Sudden Sea*, 4–5, 61–63, 127, 134–35. The annihilation of the fleet at Essex is recounted in the *Hartford Courant*, September 23, 1938.

On the New London fire, see the report from fire chief Thomas Shipman in Vol. 129 of the Hildreth Parker Collection at the Massachusetts Historical Society (hereafter cited as the Parker Collection); in Vol. 47 of the same collection is the *Quarterly of the National Fire Protection Association*, October 1938 2(2): 122–130 in Vol. 47. Other key sources are *Connecticut Circle Magazine, Photo Record: Hurricane and Flood*, November 1938, and Federal Writers' Project, *New England Hurricane*, 22–32.

On Noank, see Benjamin F. Rathbun, *Captains B. F. Rathbun of Noank* (Noank, Conn.: Noank Historical Society, 1997), 39–42, and Jerome S. Anderson III, ed., *A Matter of Minutes* (Stonington, Conn.: Stonington Publishing, 1938) 43. The story of Mrs. Orris Norman and her dog is from the PBS documentary *The Hurricane of '38*. On the Stonington train crisis, see "Fiftieth," *New Yorker*, September 19, 1988, 28–30; *Boston Post,* September 28, 1938; "Where Were You When the Big Blow Hit?," *Yankee*, September 1988, 90–91; and reports from the Red Cross and the Stonington Selectmen's Office, found in Vol. 125 of the Parker Collection.

On the flooding in inland Connecticut—especially in Hartford—see the *Hartford Courant*, September 21–23, 1938. On meteorological and flood control issues, see Vol. 58 of the Parker Collection for a Red Cross report and Vol. 60 for B. L. Bigwood, "The Hurricane Floods of September 1938 in Connecticut," *Connecticut Society of Civil Engineers Annual Report*, 1939, 137–152. On the toppling of the Wesleyan chapel, see *Wesleyan University Bulletin, Annual Report 1938–1939*, October 1939, 33(3), and *Wesleyan University Bulletin*, October 1938, 2(1), both in Vol. 73 of the Parker Collection. See also Box 4, Folder 20 of the Cady Family Papers at the Rhode Island Historical Society.

Chapter Four: Rhode Island

ON THE MOORES OF WATCH HILL, see Allen, *A Wind to Shake the World*, 160–65; Scotti, *Sudden Sea*, 175–79, 191–94; and the *Providence Bulletin*, September 23, 1938. For general destruction in South County, see Minsinger, *The 1938 Hurricane*, 50–51; Federal Writers' Project, *New England Hurricane*, 42–50; Bernard L. Gordon, ed., *Hurricane in Southern New England: An Analysis of the Great Storm of 1938* (Watch Hill, R.I.: Book and Tackle Shop, 1976), 43–46.

The stories of the tugboat *May*, Blake Hareter, and James Gamache are in an American Legion report titled "Conspicuous Service" in Vol. 59 of the Parker

Collection. The Frederick Buffum account is from Vol. 122 of the Parker Collection. On Block Island, see the *Providence Journal* from September 23, 1938, and Pamela Petro, "The Stumbling Block," *American Heritage*, September/October 1988, 114–15. The William Cawley account comes from an uncited article in *Scrapbooks of Newspaper Clippings of the Rhode Island Hurricane, 1938*, a two-volume collection assembled by William J. Briston and held in the Rhode Island Collection at the Providence Public Library. The Burchill and Bliven stories are from the *Providence Bulletin* on September 23, 1938. The Mee story is from the *Westerly Sun* on September 23, 1938. Helen Joy Lee's tale is in Minsinger, *The 1938 Hurricane*, 53–58.

The story of the windblown two-year-old in The Outlet is from *In the Wake of '38*, a 1977 oral history of Rhode Island survivors by the Rhode Island Committee for the Humanities and South Kingston High School, housed in the Rhode Island Collection at the Providence Public Library. Van Wyck Mason's account of the hurricane in Providence is in the *New York Times*, September 24, 1938. On the course of the storm surge up Narragansett Bay, see Federal Writers' Project, *New England Hurricane*, 52–60.

On the flooding of downtown Providence, see the *Providence Journal*, September 22–25 and October 8, 1938; *Providence Bulletin,* September 22–23, 1938; Folder 554 in the David Patten Papers at the Rhode Island Historical Society; *The Great Hurricane and Tidal Wave: Rhode Island, September 21, 1938* (Providence: Providence Journal, 1938); *In the Wake of '38*, 3, 167; *New York Times*, September 24, 1938; *Boston Globe*, September 22, 1938; David Cornel DeJong, "Coming Through the Storm," *Yankee*, September 1939, 13. The story of the young women in Thompson's Restaurant is from the Flora Magnan File of the Albert T. Klyberg Collection, a compilation of interviews with hurricane survivors at the Rhode Island Historical Society. The story of Joe Fogel's and Lorraine Martin's wedding is from the PBS documentary *The Hurricane of '38* and from the *Providence Journal,* September 21, 1988.

For additional primary sources on the hurricane in Providence, see these manuscript collections at the Rhode Island Historical Society: the Richard Brown Baker Family Papers, the John Rowland Barker Papers, the Joseph W. Blaine Family Papers, the Blake Family Papers, the memoir of Robert Britt Jr., a letter by Ella Cook, the Thomas P. Hazard Papers, the diary of Marion Knowlton, the diary of Emily Paine, the David Patten Papers, the Gilbert B. and Doris Shaw Papers, the Horace S. and Natalie J. Strong Papers, and the Nellie (Woolhouse) Whiting Papers.

For general destruction on the east side of Narragansett Bay, see Federal Writers' Project, *New England Hurricane*, 72–77. The advertisement from the Kleistone Rubber Company is in Vol. 122 of the Parker Collection. For Newport, see A. Hartley G. Ward,

The Hurricane in Newport: A Graphic Story of the Storm by an Eyewitness (Newport, R.I., 1938) and the Joseph W. Blaine Family Papers at the Rhode Island Historical Society.

On the Conanicut Island bus tragedy, see Scotti, *Sudden Sea*, 173–75, 180–87, 219–24, 232–33, and Allen, *A Wind to Shake the World*, 220–24.

Chapter Five: Massachusetts and Beyond

RICHARD HAWES RECOUNTS the hurricane at Horseneck Beach in *The Hurricane at Westport Harbor: September 21, 1938* (Fall River, Mass.: Dover, 1938). James Blakney's story is in the *Fall River Herald-News*, September 23, 1938. The account of Ocean Grove is from Federal Writers' Project, *New England Hurricane*, 87. On pages 89–101, that source also details general destruction along the southern coastline, as does *1938 Hurricane Pictures, with a Brief Story and 400 Views of Destruction in New Bedford and Vicinity* (New Bedford, Mass.: Reynolds, 1939). *Hurricane Pictures of Greater Fall River*, found in Vol. 61 of the Parker Collection, tells the stories of the barge *Jess B. Shaw* and the tanker *Phoenix*.

The *New Bedford Standard-Times* on September 22, 1938, reveals the tragedies of the city's fishermen. The 1938 annual report for Mattapoisett, found in Vol. 46 of the Parker Collection, describes that town's damage. The story of Jennie Brown is in the *Fall River Herald-News*, September 22, 1938. Arthur Small's story is from the PBS documentary *The Hurricane of '38*. Everett Allen's reflections upon his first experiences with the hurricane are in *A Wind to Shake the World*, 313–14.

For Martha's Vineyard, see the *New Bedford Standard-Times* from September 22, 1938, and Houston Kenyon Jr., "The Hurricane of 1938: Chilmark's Great Trauma," *Dukes County Intelligencer*, 1994, 24–36. The story from South Beach is in Benedict Thielen, "A House by the Sea," *Yale Review*, March 1939, 521–29. The status of Cape Cod is discussed in Federal Writers' Project, *New England Hurricane*, 111.

The high waters of Buzzards Bay are detailed in Massachusetts Geodetic Survey, *Storm Tide: Hurricane of September 1938 in Massachusetts*, available at the Littauer Library at Harvard University. The stories from Woods Hole are in O. S. Strong, "The Hurricane at Penzance Point," *Collecting Net*, March 1939, 37. The story of the Jones couple in Falmouth is in Thomas Fuller, ed., *September 21, 1938: Falmouth, Cape Cod* (Falmouth, Mass.: A. N. Thomson, 1938). For the tragedy under the Bourne Bridge, see the Bourne annual report from 1938, found in Vol. 46 of the Parker Collection, and Allen, *A Wind to Shake the World*, 281–84.

For the "concerns" of Bostonians on the day of the hurricane, see the *Boston Globe* of September 21, 1938. The story of E. B. Rideout is in Vic Whitman, "Weatherman,"

The New England Galaxy 20 (2): 20–25. John Cawley, the chief operator of the Fire Alarm Division, describes the fire department's response in a report in Vol. 125 of the Parker Collection. The stories of the North End fishermen and the tug *Mildred Olsen* are both from the *Boston Globe* on September 22, 1938, as are many of the descriptions of havoc throughout the Boston area. See also Federal Writers' Project, *New England Hurricane*, 174–88. For the observations from the Blue Hill Observatory, see "Where Were You When the Big Blow Hit?," *Yankee*, September 1988, 92–93. Helen Whitley's reflections are from the Howard Sterling Whitley diaries at the Massachusetts Historical Society.

On the destruction of the environment and historic spaces, see the *Harvard Alumni Bulletin* from September 30, 1938 (Vol. 76 in the Parker Collection); Arnold Arboretum's *Bulletin of Popular Information* from October 7, 1938 (Vol. 85); the annual report from Concord for 1938 (Vol. 50); and the annual report from Groton for 1938 (Vol. 83). See also *Science*, October 7, 1938, 321–22.

For the story from Woburn, see Margaret Eastman, "The Great Hurricane," *American Heritage*, September 1998, 34–35. On North Attleboro, see *Where the 1938 Hurricane Struck in Attleboro* (Attleboro, Mass.: Attleboro Print, 1938), found in Vol. 51 in the Parker Collection. For Worcester and throughout central Massachusetts, see *Science*, December 30, 1938, 616–17 and Federal Writers' Project, *New England Hurricane*, 164–67. The quotation from William Zielinski of Lowell is from Federal Writers' Project, *New England Hurricane*, 191.

Most of the descriptions from western Massachusetts are from Federal Writers' Project, *New England Hurricane*, 133–55. Details come from the *Westfield Valley Herald* on September 29, 1938 (in Vol. 124 of the Parker Collection); "I Was There," *Yankee*, June 1999; "Where Were You When the Big Blow Hit?," *Yankee*, September 1988, 93; and *The Northfield Press*, September 30, 1938.

On the flooding in southwest New Hampshire, see Vol. 61 of the Parker Collection, which has picture books entitled *Jaffrey Flood and Hurricane: September 1938* and *It DID Happen Here!: The Flood and Hurricane of 1938*. See also Federal Writers' Project, *New England Hurricane*, 195–208; *Boston Globe,* September 23, 1938; and *Manchester Union*, September 23, 1938. The details of the Peterborough fire are from *Quarterly of the National Fire Protection Association* 2(2), October 1938, 98. The tragedy in North Weare is from the *Manchester Union* on September 22, 1938. The birth of Joan Morrison is from the *Boston Post* on September 28, 1938.

On Vermont, see Federal Writers' Project, *New England Hurricane*, 211–16, and the *Newport Daily Express* from September 22, 1938, found in Vol. 67 of the Parker Collection.

Chapter Six: Aftermath

THE RISING DEATH TOLLS are from the *Providence Journal*, September 22–24, 1938. The statistics on the hurricane's toll, including the comparison figures from other disasters, are in Allen, *A Wind to Shake the World*, 349–50. The comparison to Samuel Goldwyn's movie is from the *Providence Journal* on September 28, 1938.

Frances Woodward's quotation regarding the cleanup effort comes from her article "Wind and Fury" in *Atlantic Monthly*, December 1938, 757.

David Molloy's recollection is from the David and Miriam Molloy file in the Klyberg Collection. The pastor's quotation is from the *Providence Journal* on September 26, 1938. The Weather Bureau's reassurance is in the *Boston Globe* on September 22, 1938. The Rhode Island rumors come from the Richard Brown Baker Family Papers at the Rhode Island Historical Society.

On the looting and martial law, see DeJong, "Coming Through the Storm," 15; *In the Wake of '38*, 130; Strong, "The Hurricane at Penzance Point," 36–42; Betty Davis, "A Tragedy at Silver Beach," *Collecting Net*, March 1939, 31; *Providence Journal*, September 25, 1938; *New York Times*, September 25, 1938; *Boston Post*, September 28, 1938; *Hartford Courant*, September 27, 1938; *Providence Bulletin*, September 25, 1938.

For the storm's impact on industry, see the *Boston Post* from September 28, 1938, and the annual report for 1938 from Stonington, Connecticut in Vol. 53 of the Parker Collection. The story of the man who hanged himself is from "Where Were You When the Big Blow Hit?" *Yankee*, September 1988, 93. For more on the environmental impact, see Austin F. Hawes, *Hurricane Damaged Forests: Still an Important State Asset* (Hartford, 1939) and Diana Muir, "My Mother's Hurricane, and Further Cautions," *North American Review*, March–April 1998, 4–9.

On the response of the Red Cross, see American National Red Cross, *New York–New England Hurricane and Floods–1938*, 30–32, and an additional Red Cross report found in Vol. 58 of the Parker Collection. On the response of New Deal organizations, see the *Providence Journal* and *Boston Globe* from September 24–27, 1938. Arthur Raynor's complaint is from Quogue Historical Society, *The 1938 Hurricane as We Remember It*, Vol. II.

On previous disasters in American history, see Erik Larson, *Isaac's Storm: A Man, a Storm, and the Deadliest Hurricane in History* (New York: Vintage, 1999); Carl Smith, *Urban Disorder and the Shape of Belief: The Great Chicago Fire, the Haymarket Bomb, and the Model Town of Pullman* (Chicago: University of Chicago Press, 1995); Gordon Thomas and Max Morgan Witts, *The San Francisco Earthquake* (New York: Stein and Day, 1971).

For the nostalgia of old New England after the hurricane, see Colton, "Geography of a Hurricane," 529–31. On the timber crisis, see the report from the New Hampshire State Park and Forest Commission in Vol. 63 of the Parker Collection. On transportation snafus and the use of airlines, see the *Boston Globe* of September 22–23, 1938, and Federal Writers' Project, *New England Hurricane*, 218–19. The quotation from New Haven Railroad authorities is from www.gis.net/~wreidy/htdocs/images0998.

On the response of the Post Office, see the *Boston Post*, September 27, 1938.

On the response of the telephone and power companies, see E. C. Schnurmacher, "Challenges of Disaster," *Popular Mechanics*, May 1939, 723–25; "Hurricane Damage and Repairs to Bristol, R.I., Water Works," *American City*, December 1938, 64–65; Ralph W. Eaton, "Reconditioning a Wrecked City," *American City*, January 1939, 83–84. See also the publications of the New England Power Association, the New England Telephone and Telegraph Company, and the Southern New England Telegraph Company, found throughout the Parker Collection.

The aftermath in Quogue, Long Island, is discussed throughout Quogue Historical Society, *The 1938 Hurricane as We Remember It*, Vol. II. Harrison McDonald's experience in New London is in the PBS documentary *The Hurricane of '38*. The portrait of Hartford is from the *Hartford Courant* on September 23–27, 1938 and Tyler, *The New England Hurricane*, 42. For Harold Kenyon's recollections from Westerly, see *In the Wake of '38*, found in the Rhode Island Collection of the Providence Public Library. The appropriations of the Massachusetts state legislature are found in Vols. 55 and 59 of the Parker Collection. On the aftermath in western Massachusetts, see Federal Writers' Project, *New England Hurricane*, 129–131, and *Boston Post*, September 26, 1938. The headline of the *Peterborough Transcript* is from September 22, 1938. Fairfax Downey's story is in his article "Neighbors," found in *The Commentator*, January 1939, 65–69.

The day-by-day course of the Czechoslovakian crisis and its obscuring of the hurricane is best seen through the *New York Times* in the weeks following September 21, 1938.

On the rebuilding of churches and the search for the hurricane's meaning, see the church pamphlets in Vols. 69, 122, and 139 in the Parker Collection.

INDEX